MODERN ENGLISH MISUSAGE

For all those souls who were personally challenged
by the author to speak the King's English properly,
and for all others who missed that rare opportunity.

MODERN ENGLISH MISUSAGE

THE RULES OF GRAMMAR, EXPLAINED WITH PRECISION AND WIT

BY BARNEY OLIVER

ILLUSTRATED BY HERB STANSBURY

MOUNTAIN VIEW, CALIFORNIA

SETI Press
Seth Shostak, Managing Editor
SETI Institute
2035 Landings Drive
Mountain View, CA 94043
www.SETI.org

Manufactured in the United States of America.
ISBN: 0-9666335-1-2 (Special Memorial Edition)

Publisher's Cataloging-in-Publication
(Provided by Quality Books, Inc.)

Oliver, Bernard M., 1916–
 Modern English misusage : the rules of grammar,
 explained with precision and wit / by Barney Oliver ;
 illustrated by Herb Stansbury. — 1st ed.
  p. cm.
  Includes bibliographical references and index.
  ISBN: 0-9666335-2-0

 1. English language—Errors of usage. 2. English
language—Grammar. I. Title.

PE1460.O45 2001   428.2
            QBI01-200493

PRODUCTION CREDITS

COVER DESIGN / GRAPHIC DESIGN AND PRODUCTION
 Russell Leong Design, Palo Alto, California

PROJECT MANAGER/EDITOR
 Dona M. LeyVa

PRODUCTION EDITOR
 Karen M. Shibata

COPY EDITOR
 Robert Haas

INDEXER
 J. Naomi Linzer

PROOFREADERS
 Ann Behrman; Lee Engfer

PRINTING
 Courier Co., Westford, Massachusetts

PHOTO CREDITS

Back cover – *Courtesy of Hewlett-Packard Co.*
Inside back cover flap – *Courtesy of Herb Stansbury*
p. 95 – *Courtesy of Hewlett-Packard Co.*
p. 101, top, center, – *Courtesy of Oliver family archive,
 SETI Institute*
p. 101, bottom – *Courtesy of Hewlett-Packard Co.*
p. 102, top, bottom – *Courtesy of Hewlett-Packard Co.*
p. 103, top, bottom – *Courtesy of Hewlett-Packard Co.*
p. 104, top – *Courtesy of Seth Shostak, SETI Institute*
p. 104, bottom – *Courtesy of SETI Institute*

EARLY DEVELOPMENT

EDITORIAL REVIEW
 Ted Michel

DESIGN CONCEPTS
 Rich Wallace

Acknowledgments

The SETI Institute was deeply honored to receive this exceptional volume as part of Barney Oliver's estate. The challenge was to convert the manuscript into an actual publication. The Institute owes a debt of gratitude to Herb Stansbury, who not only provided the exceptional illustrations, but also worked with the Institute's John Billingham and Greg Klerkx to arrange for proper sponsorship of Barney's book. The idea was proposed to Walter Hewlett, then gained a solid nod from his father, Bill Hewlett. The SETI Institute and SETI Press are truly indebted to The William R. Hewlett Revocable Trust for providing the funds to bring this book to life.

The book would not have emerged to print without the tireless efforts of editor Dona LeyVa and production editor Karen Shibata, as well as the Managing Editor of SETI Press, Seth Shostak, and Shannon Atkinson, Vera Buescher, Debbie Kolyer, Michelle Murray, Chris Neller, and Hal Roey of the SETI Institute.

It is a humbling experience to be handed this kind of treasure from such a gifted friend, and no one is more pleased than I to know the joy that will come from spreading Barney's wit and wisdom far and wide.

Tom Pierson
Chief Executive Officer
SETI Institute
Mountain View, California

TABLE OF CONTENTS

   Plurals of Nouns from the Latin or Greek
      Table I: Common Words of Latin Origin
      Table II: Common Words of Greek Origin
   Proper Nouns
   Possessive Nouns and Pronouns
   Computer Spelling-Checkers
   Gerunds
   Some Troublesome Nouns

   Split Infinitives
   Moods or Modes
   Capricious Nonsense
   Some Problem Verbs

   Comparison of Adjectives and Adverbs
   Predicate Adjectives and Verbs of Perception
   Misused Modifiers

INTRODUCTION

C amping near Monte Rio, California, eighty-five miles north of San Francisco, Barney and I sat next to a campfire on a chilly midnight in late July. We were sipping small amounts of Cardhu single malt and nibbling on pistachio nuts while having a fine conversation. Barney had been leading our discussion. That was normal.

On this night, our agenda included the search for extraterrestrial intelligence (SETI), Jack London, Kipling, Langdon Smith, Galileo, and how computers have revolutionized time orientation (just as the invention of clocks did several hundred years earlier and the ringing of bells by Benedictine monks before that).

Eventually we got to our favorite subject—the English language. Above all, Barney wanted men, women, and children to express themselves clearly and succinctly.

For an hour, we laughed at the language of anchorpersons and sports announcers, who so frequently butcher their grammar. We also made fun of boomers as well as some prominent Silicon Valley executives who occasionally have trouble with simple sixth-grade grammar, especially the subjunctive mode.

"I want our language to preserve its ability to convey efficiently the subtlest shades of meaning. It's a beautiful language. Let's do it justice," Barney emphasized over and over.

"The fire is almost out, Herb. Shall we put on another log and have one more nip of Cardhu?" A good idea, but it was getting late, almost 2:30 A.M., and we decided

to skip the nightcap and get some sleep. Barney's final comment was, "I'll show you my book manuscript tomorrow."

The next morning, before breakfast, Barney pulled *Modern English Misusage* out of his bag, a neatly typed manuscript in a blue Hewlett-Packard three-ring binder. "Take it home, look it over, and determine if you'd like to illustrate it with your cartoons. There's a lot of script. I think it needs your comic relief and maybe some editing. Would that be an imposition? You'll be my partner?"

Was I flattered? You bet! I took the manuscript home, read it with magnum enthusiasm, and sketched several cartoons for the first chapter. Barney was tickled with my efforts, which I showed him the following week at his SETI Institute headquarters in Mountain View.

Then, sadly, and without much warning, Barney died. I thought the project had gone with him until John Billingham phoned me a few weeks later and explained that Barney had left *Modern English Misusage* to the SETI Institute. John hoped that I would stay with the project, finish the cartoons, and help get his book published. And that's how we got to where we are now.

HERB STANSBURY

PREFACE

During my forty-odd years as a practicing electrical engineer, I became increasingly well known for my habit of correcting people's English on the fly. *Notorious* is perhaps a better word. *Renowned* would never do. This impolite practice was seldom accepted as gracefully by the victim as I felt it should have been.

Instead of seizing on the correct form with proper gratitude, the speaker would often stop mid-sentence in puzzlement or even consternation, exhibiting a growing resentment over the interruption. In later years, realizing that fewer people smiled at me or hailed me by my first name, I took to murmuring the necessary corrections several times, rapidly and barely audibly. This, of course, did the speaker no good. It only bothered those nearby, and the chairman, who thought an unwelcome caucus was in progress. I did, however, continue to satisfy a mysterious compulsion within me. I was still giving Mama the correct answer. How well I remember that formidable lady. In the teacher shortage after World War I, she was drafted back into the classroom. She solved the babysitting problem by taking me along. It was

understood that I would sit quietly in the wood box, next to the stove, and listen to all eight grades recite. But if I elected to join the first grade, I had better perform. There was to be no favoritism! U.C. Berkeley had not only given my mother a master's degree in history, it had instilled in her an evangelical zeal for correct English. She saw no reason why her new charges should not perform to high school standards. As a result, her Temple of Learning was no elementary school; it was an advanced grammar school. Thus I came to read and reckon at the age of four. School has been downhill ever since.

THE DAY LITTLE BARNEY ACCIDENTALLY SAID "LIBARY"

To make sure I wouldn't embarrass her with my innocent speech, she took to correcting me not only at school, but during all my conscious hours. I gained a teacher but lost a mother. So my only excuse for my pernicious habit is that it is hereditary.

Perhaps not genetic, but hereditary nevertheless. I am the product of incessant correction. Why should you find life so easy?

Seriously, I don't think incessant correction is the answer. And to give Mother her due, she did a great deal more than merely correct. She taught the rules, and not just to me. Those were the years when public education was a dream come true. It was young, vigorous, and its practitioners were not afraid to teach. They had the naive idea that that was what they were paid for, and they gave full measure. Some gave much more than their meager pay warranted.

Today it has become the fashion to denigrate the teaching of plain factual knowledge, the kind that gives kids the background and skills to contribute to the world. If you really want to be what is now called an "educator," you eschew all such teaching. Instead, you instill in your flock the *desire* to learn. How to do this without actually teaching something rewarding in the process requires a great deal of training that can only be acquired in the best schools of education. Certainly, motivation is

WE DON'T SPEND YEARS MOTIVATING OUR ATHLETES. WE TEACH THEM THE SKILLS AND STRATEGY OF THE GAME AND THEN PRACTICE, PRACTICE, PRACTICE.

important in education, but so is content. What better motivation can the student have than the thrill of success, to discover that she or he has acquired new skills and new understanding?

We don't spend years motivating our athletes. We teach them the skills and strategy of the game and then practice, practice, practice. The reward comes in the play-off, especially if we are good enough to win. We'd have more mental athletes if we taught reading, writing, reckoning, and all the rest this same way.

Whatever the cause, there seems to be an increasing number of people who have difficulty with the most fundamental skill of all: communication in their native tongue. Sometimes the errors are in spelling, but more often they are in grammar or usage. Often they betray a desire to speak correctly, as when someone says, "I feel badly about that." Feel is a verb, isn't it? And adverbs modify verbs, don't they? And adding -ly makes an adverb, so what's wrong? What's wrong is that no one taught the speaker about copulation! If that surprises you, you may enjoy this book. It's not about sex, but it does talk about certain verbs called *copulas* and why they require adjectives.

I've tried to include the most common errors I find in today's speech and writing. At the same time, I've tried to keep the book short. These apparently conflicting aims mean that I've not included a lot of items that guardians of the language object to.

FOOTBALL ANNOUNCERS, ESPECIALLY FORMER LINEMEN, ARE OFTEN CONFUSED BY THE SUBJUNCTIVE.

I don't mind ending sentences with prepositions, in most cases. In fact, I just did. I don't care if you occasionally split infinitives, or use the word "hopefully." But I do care if you aren't familiar with the subjunctive mode and say, "I would have . . ." instead of "Had I . . ." I do want you to use pronouns correctly. Above all, I do want you to know how to express yourself clearly and succinctly. I'm not trying to resist change and prevent further evolution of English; quite the contrary. But I want our language to preserve its ability to convey efficiently the subtlest shades of meaning. It's a beautiful language. Let's do it justice.

BARNEY OLIVER

All animals, ourselves included, exhibit distinctive behavior. Birds use themselves as decoys to lure predators from their nests. Squirrels hide nuts in old trees as food for the winter. Occasionally, a chimpanzee is coaxed into devising and using tools, as when it climbs on a box and uses a stick to break a banana from the bunch hanging in its cage. Many animals have cries, calls,

or songs that appear to have meaning. But these are isolated utterances intended to warn, locate, or seduce other animals of their kind. We appear to be the only species on earth that uses concatenations of individually meaningful words to express thoughts of far greater variety and complexity. We call it speaking, and we call what is spoken and its rules a language.

We are the only terrestrial species with a language. (Whales and dolphins may be linguists, but it's doubtful.) The consequences of that simple fact are

enormous. The amount of true Darwinian evolution that has taken place since ancient times is probably negligible—at least so small that many people don't believe it exists. Actually, the amount of true genetic evolution over historical time may be negative. Yet the increase in human knowledge during that same instant in geologic time has been astonishing.

Langdon Smith[1] reminds us how at the dawn of history:

Deep in the gloom of a fireless cave,
When the night fell o'er the plain
And the moon hung red o'er the river bed
We mumbled the bones of the slain.

Now we have landed on that moon. We have vanquished many diseases that once beset the human race. We have measured the size and age of the universe and are close to learning how it all began.

None of this marvelous progress has been taught to us. No book of revelation reveals a table of isotopes, or, for that matter, uses the word. Instead, we are beneficiaries of cultural evolution: of the enormous increase in our capabilities that accrues from communication, from working on parts of a problem and then pooling our results, and from transmitting all we know from generation to generation as a growing wave of human understanding. In this process, language plays a central and essential role.

It is because language is so important to civilization that some of us treasure it and hate to see it abused. Anything so important to our lives, we feel, should be treated with respect and mastered as a tool. Not only does this increase our own effectiveness, but it also increases our appreciation and enjoyment of the words of others.

This book, like all instruction books, is full of admonitions: say this, this is right, don't say that, that's wrong. So many admonitions that you could be forgiven resenting the whole business and turning to the sports pages. Or maybe you are now ready to take a more mature look at the matter? In any case, I don't want to lose you before I can set the hook, so I'd better explain a couple of things right away.

In the first place, I really shouldn't say "right" and "wrong," for these words have strong moral overtones for many people. Instead, I should really say (and sometimes do) "correct" and "incorrect." So relax. You will not fry in hell if you say "the book *laid* there all week." Nor will you win eternal bliss

by saying "it has *lain* there all week." We are just pointing out the rules of the game, not issuing ten thousand commandments. I switch words now and then because I dislike repetition. That's one reason for synonyms.

It is a truism that languages change with time. The ferment of life brews new thoughts to be expressed and needs new words to name new things. Slowly, established usage gives way to a new mode as the latter proves its worth in brevity and clarity. Is it then any surprise that the admonitions expressed in books like this change also? If I say it is okay to split infinitives (if you don't split them too far) and to decorate the ends of your sentences with prepositions, and you find some grammarian (perhaps your English teacher) who regards such acts as

unforgivable, does that make one of us wrong? Probably. But usage changes over the years. The modern view is to eschew rules that restrict words unnecessarily. The point is that there is no absolute set of rules for grammar guaranteed to last forever.

E.B. White,[2] the revered essayist of *The New Yorker* magazine, says:

The living language is like a cowpath: it is the creation of the cows themselves, who, having created it, follow it or depart from it according to their whims and needs. From daily use, the path undergoes change. A cow is under no obligation to stay in the narrow path she helped make, following the contour of the road, but she often profits by staying with it, and she would be handicapped if she didn't know where it was or where it led to. Children obviously do not depend for communication on a knowledge of grammar; they rely on their ear, mostly, which is sharp and quick. But we have yet to see the child who has not profited from coming face to face with a relative pronoun at an early age, and from reading books, which follow the paths of centuries.

But just as it is impossible to prevent change, so, too, it is folly to accept all change or, in desperation, to abandon all rules. For then there are no established routes to guide us. We need all the help we can get to write well. The job of guardian of the mother tongue, which some of us seem called upon to perform, is to decide which set of rules will work best and will endure. For that is all we are thinking about: *the rules of the game.*

We do not seem to appreciate this simple fact: The same student who disrupts his English class, challenges the teacher's right to correct usage, and spends his time either sleeping or busily rejecting his lesson (the old-fashioned word for a "learning experience") can be found that afternoon wincing at but enduring the criticism of his football coach.

And having listened, he tries harder and eventually succeeds. Why this dichotomy? Or take a music class. Who dares challenge the teacher's right to insist on proper tempo and intonation? We've all heard bands without these and don't want to hear them again.

The rules of grammar are just as important as those of music and other arts. Surely they change, but so do others. Yes, they are somewhat arbitrary, but not as much as you would think.

Mastering our language—our native tongue—is the single most important skill we learn. Let's try to communicate rather than confuse the listener. Let's do it right. It's not that hard.

Look, I'm the umpire. I get to call the shots. These are The Top Nine Offenders because I say so. They include the improper use of:

1. *Myself* in place of *I* or *me*.
2. *Lay* for *lie*.
3. I feel *badly* instead of I feel *bad*.
4. *Like* for *as*.
5. The media *is* instead of the media *are*.
6. *At this point in time* instead of *now*.
7. *Anxious* instead of *eager*.
8. *Less* for *fewer*.
9. *If I would have* in place of *had I*.

The list may change next week, but it is my list right now. If you have a better one, please send it to the publishers. Who is to say what the most frequent misuses are? Nobody keeps count. Besides, frequency is not the only criterion. Seriousness, in the sense of potential for weakening the language, is certainly another. So is the size of the implied area of confusion in the speaker's mind. So what do I mean by The Top Nine Offenders? Simply the gaffes that bother me the most.

1 | By all odds, the biggest speech problem today is the misuse of pronouns. It betrays a general ignorance of the elementary matter of case.

For number one I nominate: **The use of *myself* in place of *I* or *me*.**

Runner-ups are **the use of *I* instead of *me*, and vice versa.** (See Chapter 6, "Me, Myself, and I, or: The Great Pronoun Mess.")

2 | The persistent use of the transitive verb *lay* instead of the proper intransitive *lie* continues to assail our ears. For second place (with a blue ribbon for endurance) I nominate: **The use of *lay* for *lie*.** The use of *lie* for *lay*, equally wrong, is less common. (See Chapter 4, "Verbs: Where the Action Is.")

3 | Of the many misuses of adverbs, I single out for third place the venerable: **I feel *badly*.** Along with **That dress looks *well* on you,** this one may have passed its peak. Let's hope so. (See Chapter 5, "The Modifiers: Adjectives and Adverbs.")

4 | My nominee for fourth place is another oldie: **The improper use of *like* for *as*.** We have a test for this problem that may knock it out of The Top Nine, if all goes well. (See Chapter 7, "Some Elements of Syntax.")

5 | Among the vogue words today, *media* is enjoying huge popularity. Since the word is the plural of *medium*, I dislike its singular use and nominate **the media *is*** for fifth place. I hope **the media *are*** happy about this. (See Chapter 3, "Nouns and Articles.")

6 | A relative newcomer makes its appearance in sixth place: **At this point in time.** Actually, I nominate this whole phrase for oblivion, along with *due to the fact that* and others of its ilk. (See Chapter 7, "Some Elements of Syntax.")

7 | Adjectives take another spot. For seventh place: **The use of *anxious* instead of *eager.*** This might be called grammatical overacting. Most of the time you're merely eager. Don't ham it up. (See Chapter 5, "The Modifiers: Adjectives and Adverbs.")

8 | Hanging in year after year like a nasal drip in eighth place: **The use of *less* for *fewer*.** (See Chapter 5, "The Modifiers: Adjectives and Adverbs.")

9 | In ninth place, I would put the awkward: *if I would have* used in place of *had I.* Come on, save the subjunctive. (See Chapter 4, "Verbs: Where the Action Is.")

ALAN J. LERNER GOT IT WRONG.

No doubt you have your own pet peeves you feel belong to The Top Nine. We invite you to send them to the publishers, and perhaps they will become part of our next edition. If not a kinder, gentler America, maybe we can look forward to a more grammatical one.

Almost twenty years ago, my friend of Bell Laboratories days, Harald Friis, suffered a stroke that left him with a serious but temporary aphasia. Remarkably, his loss of verbal recall was limited to nouns. We've all forgotten a proper

I'VE GOT ALL MY ADJECTIVES AND ADVERBS... BUT NO NOUNS.

HARALD'S APHASIA LIMITED HIS LOSS OF VERBAL RECALL TO NOUNS.

name or two at times, but suddenly to lose all nouns and only nouns implies that they were all stored in the same, now damaged, region of Harald's brain. When I excitedly described this nugget of information to my neurologist friends, I was told that the phenomenon was well known. Moral: Don't expect credit for finding gold in other people's mines.

Old hat or not, the discovery that nature files words away in our heads under the same classifications used by the Romans confers a certain authenticity on these Latin parts of speech. Somehow, the classification must relate to our thinking process, which suggests we should understand classical sentence structure no matter what new transformational grammars may come our way.

Nouns are the names of the things we are talking about in a sentence. In English, nouns are often preceded by the definite article *the* or the indefinite article *a* or *an*. *The* house means a particular house, one we have already mentioned or will shortly describe, whereas *a* house means any house. The names of specific people, places, planets, etc., are called **proper nouns**, and their initial letters are capitalized.

Compared with those of most other languages, English nouns and their articles are models of simplicity. For one thing, they are not **inflected**; that is, they do not change their form depending on their role in the sentence. *The boy* remains *the boy* whether he is the subject of the verb or its direct or indirect object. Not so, abroad. And, to make

THE BOY REMAINS THE BOY WHETHER HE IS THE SUBJECT OF THE VERB OR ITS DIRECT OR INDIRECT OBJECT.

matters worse, the nouns over there come in two or three types, called **genders**. In German, for example, there are three genders and a plural, each with its own schedule of articles for four cases. As *aüslander* we must decide before speaking each noun which of the sixteen possible combinations applies, and then choose the proper *der, die, das, des, dem,* or *den.* What a waste of time over a tiny

article! We still **decline** our pronouns in English, and seeing what a mess we make of the restrictive pronoun *that,* be glad we don't decline our nouns as well. (See Glossary of Grammatical Terms, page 78.)

The word *gender* once meant *kind* or *sort* (compare with *genre*) and was introduced into linguistics to describe classifications of nouns according to which articles they took. Because these classifications are called masculine, feminine, and neuter, it was inevitable that the word *gender* would come to be used as a synonym for sex—or rather, sexual category. All this amuses the German who says *der wein* or *das weib* not because he thinks *wine* is male (he doesn't) or that his *wife* is neuter (he'd better not!), but because those articles sound right. Our extension of this meaning of the word *gender* is certain to stimulate many letters to the editor,

but it is hardly objectionable on grammatical grounds. Fowler[3] would probably call it a "genteelism," which he defines as "rejecting of the ordinary natural word that first suggests itself to the mind, and the substitution of a synonym thought to be less soiled by the lips of the common herd, less familiar, less plebeian, less vulgar, less improper, less apt to come unhandsomely betwixt the wind and our nobility." There is however, little doubt that *sex* is overworked as a word as well as a topic. Perhaps we do need a genteel synonym.

With **inflection** and **gender** eliminated, what else can go wrong with nouns? There's not much left except the way we form their **plurals**. For the bulk of our nouns, we simply add *-s* or *-es* as the pronunciation demands. We remember, or our spell-check reminds us, that the final *-y* generally turns to *-ies,* as in *sky, skies.* We know about the irregular plurals like *children, geese, mice, oxen, teeth,* and *women* and also about the words that don't change, like *sheep, deer, trout,* and *Chinese.* We actually handle the plurals of our own English words fairly well. We find an occasional person who is convinced that *species* (as in Darwin) is plural. He drops the final *s* to form the singular and finds himself talking about gold or silver coins. But such cases are rare.

Some confusion exists over the formation of the plural of compound nouns. If the recipe calls for one tablespoon of sugar and you have only a teaspoon at hand, should you add three *teaspoonsful* or three *teaspoonfuls*? The answer in this case is to ask yourself which is plural, the *spoons* or the *fillings?* I suggest you would probably plunge your single teaspoon into the sugar three times and dump its contents into your cake mix each time. Thus, the *fillings* are plural and the word you want is *teaspoonfuls.*

Of course, you may be giving cough medicine to triplets and, mindful of preventing contagion, you have lined up three teaspoons and filled each one once with sweet, sticky goo. Now, Dr. Mom or Dad, you are giving three *teaspoonsful* of medicine to your brood. But mostly we need the word *teaspoonfuls.*

Plurals of Nouns from the Latin or Greek

Where we really seem to fall apart is in forming or recognizing the plurals of words of Latin or Greek origin for which we still use the original, unanglicized form. In the early days of public education, this was no problem; most college-bound students took Latin in high school and sometimes Greek as well. Today, we go in for bilingual education, which doesn't mean teaching English to immigrant children as was intended. It means teaching Spanish poorly in elementary grades and displacing the normal English classes. No problem, we just teach the English in high school, when it's too late, and it displaces the classics. Don't you understand

modern high-tech educational planning? In any event, the classics have almost disappeared from high school and, to a great extent, from college curricula as well. Today, almost all that most graduates can recall is *one radius, many radii.*

To help you hang on to some guideposts during this U.S. cultural revolution, we have included Tables I and II showing common English words of Latin and Greek origin, respectively. For many of these words, we have anglicized plurals in common use: *antennas, formulas, appendixes, dogmas, viruses,* to name a few. Whether you use these or the original plural forms is largely a matter of taste. Many of the classic plurals are shorter, and for that reason preferable. The real trouble is that many people mistake the plural forms for the singular and try to make super-plurals of an already plural noun. Thus we hear "how many *agendas* (copies of the agenda) do you have" or "there are a great many *criterias* one can use here." Well, I'm going to use mine: Get it right!

Probably the champion offender in this class is *media*, referring to all our means of communication: television, radio, motion pictures, newspapers, and magazines. So many people now think *media* is singular that we'll probably never recover, but here goes: *Media* is plural. *These are the news media.* The word *medium* means more than what you want your steak to be rarer than. Besides meaning *not extreme*, it is the singular of *media*. There it means the substance or mechanism through which a force acts or an effect is transmitted.

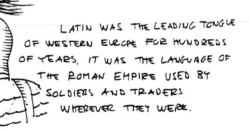

TABLE I
Common Words of Latin Origin

Singular	Plural	Singular	Plural
alga	algae	curriculum	curricula
alumna(f)	alumnae	datum	data
antenna	antennae	emporium	emporia
formula	formulae	erratum	errata
larva	larvae	medium	media
minutia	minutiae	memorandum	memoranda
alumnus(m)	alumni	orum	ora
cactus	cacti	stratum	strata
focus	foci	corpus	corpora
fungus	fungi	genus	genera
radius	radii	opus	opera
apex	apices	axis	axes
appendix	appendices	crux	cruces
index	indices	dux	duces
matrix	matrices	pons	pontes
addendum	addenda	rex	reges
agendum	agenda	nexus	nexus
aquarium	aquaria	nomer	nomina
bacterium	bacteria	series	series

GREEK IS ONE OF THE OLDEST SURVIVING BRANCHES OF THE INDO-EUROPEAN FAMILY OF LANGUAGES. IT IS RELATED TO LATIN, HITTITE, OLD SLAVIC, CELTIC, AND THE GERMANIC LANGUAGES.

TABLE II
Common Words of Greek Origin

Singular	Plural	Singular	Plural
analysis	analyses	carcinoma	carcinomata
basis	bases	dogma	dogmata
crisis	crises	lemma	lemmata
ellipsis	ellipses	miasma	miasmata
genesis	geneses	schema	schemata
nemesis	nemeses	aphis	aphides
parenthesis	parentheses	ephemeris	ephemerides
thesis	theses	iris	irides
automaton	automata	cyclops	cyclopes
criterion	criteria	larynx	larynges
ephemeron	ephemera	phalanx	phalanges
ganglion	ganglia	sphinx	sphinges
phenomenon	phenomena	logos	logoi

Also, by extension, "medium" means anything by which something else is accomplished, such as an advertising *medium*. It used to be thought that light was a vibration in an elastic substance. The *medium*, which had to be incredibly light and rigid, was called the *luminiferous* (light-carrying) *ether*. Now, physicists no longer speak of the ether, but astronomers still refer to the *interstellar medium* as the purveyor of all their information. The tape on which you store the voices and images of your dear ones is a recording *medium*. Back in the days when belief in magic was not confined to actress Shirley MacLaine, the psychic through whom messages allegedly came from "the other side" was called a *medium*. *Medium* also means *not extreme*, but that takes us back to our steak, which is now cold, so let's move on. Before doing so, however, would you please write *"one medium, many media"* twenty-five times? Then go around saying the phrase to yourself for a few days.

A difference seldom observed these days is that between *alumna*, a female graduate, and *alumnus*, a male graduate. Their plurals, respectively, are *alumnae*, pronounced *alum-nee*, and *alumni*, pronounced *alum-nigh*.

For some words with an accepted anglicized plural, the Latin plural tends to take on a different meaning. An example is *stadium*. In surveying, distances are sometimes given by the apparent difference in height on the image of the *stadia* rod in the surveyor's eyepiece of two parallel, horizontal *stadia* crosshairs. The word has a long pedigree in distance measurement. Eratosthenes, in about 250 B.C., noticed that on a certain day, when the sun made a 7° angle to the vertical at noon in Alexandria, it was directly overhead in Syene, 4860 *stadia* due south. He therefore concluded that the circumference of the earth was 360 x 4860/7, or roughly 250,000 *stadia* in circumference. Unfortunately, we don't really know how long his unit of length, the *stadium*, really is. Many believe it to be the distance between the start and finish lines of the racetrack in front of the reviewing stands at the stadium at Mount Olympus. If so, Eratosthenes hit it right on the mark, for that distance is 1/10 mile. In any event, Eratosthenes earned his spot in history not by merely accepting along with other Alexandrians that the earth is a sphere, but by having the courage of his convictions and actually measuring its size.

Proper Nouns

A **proper noun** is the name of a person, place, or an institution or thing of singular importance. *Charles, Chicago, Earth,* and the *Library of Congress* are examples. Proper nouns are always capitalized. Astronomers capitalize our *Galaxy,* but not other galaxies. Similarly, *Earth* is capitalized when we mean our *Earth,* but not when we mean any habitable planet or the ground beneath us. The capitalization of titles is too complex and too rarely a problem for us to cover here. Consult your reference library.

Possessive Nouns and Pronouns

Possessives of singular nouns are formed by adding *'s*. There is some indication that the elided letters were originally *h* and *i*. Thus, on old maps we may find *Hudson, his Bay,* while on later additions *Hudson's Bay* is the rule. There is a common belief that for words ending in *s*, the final *s* after the apostrophe should be dropped. On the other hand, Will Strunk in *The Elements of Style*[4] begins page 1 with the recommended examples:

> *Charles's friend*
> *Burns's poems*
> *the witch's malice*

These seem fine to me. The problem appears to arise when there are too many sibilants in a row at the end of the word. Thus, *for Jesus's sake* ends up with a double *zuzz zuzz* at the end, which is too much, so we write and say *for Jesus' sake.* It is a question of pronounceability and grace. So base your choice on the sound. But don't leave off the final *s* in the writing and expect the speaker to say it in the reading! Conversely, don't expect the reader to delete an *'s* that is there.

Perhaps the evolution of *'s* from *his* is to blame, or perhaps it's the thought that only humans and animals can truly possess something else, but the apostrophal possessive is less frequently used with inanimate nouns. We speak of the *radius of the circle,* the *beat of a tom-tom,* the *call of the wild.* In many cases, the short apostrophal form is possible, but sound it out and proceed with caution.

Personal pronouns in the possessive case *(ours, yours, theirs)* do not require the apostrophe. Nothing has been elided. On the other hand, apostrophes are sometimes used to indicate unusual plurals such as:

There are four *s's*, four *i's*, and two *p's* in Mississippi. He continually confused his *that's* and *which's*.

Computer Spelling-Checkers

With the advent of the personal computer, it has become common to rely upon the spell-check routines of the word-processor program to catch typos and other misspellings. These programs are good at finding errors like omitted or interchanged letters that produce gibberish, but they cannot detect errors that produce other words, especially words that you might be using. This fault is likely to show up in the substitution of one homophone for another: *forward* for *foreword* for example, or *principle* for *principal*. Of course, there's always a

possibility that some human along the way may have been responsible, but let's never admit *that*. Let's do what everyone does: blame the computer.

You may be in awe of them, but the truth is that the poor little things don't understand anything you're saying. They can only do what their absentee masters, the programmers, have taught them to do. You must develop a professional, clinical attitude toward them if you are to maintain your own sanity.

Gerunds

English is noted for the ease with which one part of speech can be used as another part of speech: nouns used as verbs, verbs used as nouns, nouns as adjectives, and so on. Many grammarians are bothered by each new usage of this sort, and indeed it must be done with care to avoid derailing the reader. As bad examples I offer the use, by computer gurus, of the words *input* and *output*, normally nouns, in sentences like *The data are first input to the cache memory* or *The results are output on demand*. They could say the data are first *put into* the cache memory, and the results are *put out* on demand, but somehow this makes the operation too plain.

Nevertheless, this freedom to use a word as any of several parts of speech is very useful. It eliminates having to invent new words. We do it so often that some of the cases are given special names. A noun used as an adjective is called an **attributive noun**. In *Down by the old mill stream, mill* is an attributive noun. Maybe you have heard of gerunds and, like many people, have been afraid of being introduced to some obscure principle of grammar that you'd never use. It's not that way at all. A **gerund** is the present participle of a verb used as a noun, and you use them every day.

Parting is the present participle of the verb *to part.* In *"Parting is such sweet sorrow,"* Shakespeare used it as a noun. You do it, too. You say *Swimming is good exercise,* or *Acting develops the ability to view oneself objectively.* Meet the gerund! He's an old friend of yours.

A participle used as an adjective is called a **gerundive.** We speak of a *skiing instructor* or a *dancing partner. Skiing* and *dancing* are used here as adjectives and are called gerundives.

Some Troublesome Nouns

English is full of noun pairs that are spelled nearly alike but have distinct meanings or implications. Books about these "confusables" are available[5,6,7] and are perhaps second only to a dictionary in usefulness to the careful writer.

accessory, accessary | There is a vanishing distinction between these two words, both of which mean *a useful addition.* An *accessary* was a person assisting in an act, as an *accessary to a crime.* An *accessory* was an attachment to extend the usefulness of a primary item, such as a flash attachment for a camera, or even gloves to match your shoes.

adherence, adhesion | Both words mean *to cling,* but the first implies devotion to an idea or principle, the second the literal sticking of one thing to another, as tires to the road.

alternate, alternative | Pronounced *ALL-ter-nate,* an *alternate* (noun) is a person who can act for another, as in playing a role in a theater production. An *all-TERN-ative* is a second choice.

ante-, anti- | These prefixes for nouns sound almost alike unless you stress the final short vowel, which I recommend. Their meanings are quite distinct. *Ante-* means *before* or *prior to,* as in *anteroom* (a room before the main one) or *antedeluvian* (before the flood). *Anti-* means opposed to, as in *antisocial* (opposed to society) or *antipodes (an-TIP-o-deez),* the portions of the earth diametrically opposed to our feet.

astrology, astronomy | Both words come from the Greek *astron,* meaning *star.* Coupled with *logos,* meaning *the logic of* or *discourse on, astrology* meant the science of the stars. Coupled with *nemein—to distribute or arrange—astronomy* meant *the study of stellar arrangements and configurations.* In the days of magic, before Newton, the wanderings of the planets among the fixed stars were thought to influence the destinies of men, and astrology was considered an important, albeit mysterious, study. Now that these wanderings are explained as merely the view of the solar system as seen from our own moving planet, the exhortations of astrologers are considered baseless except by those who prefer myth to mastery of their own destiny. By contrast, astronomy has emerged as the true science and the science we hope will answer the questions of how it all began. To lose an astronomer as a friend, call him an astrologer.

auger, augur | An *auger* is a tool for boring. Not to be confused with the verb *augur*, which means *portend*. (Warning: If *auger* is followed by the word *spectroscopy*, give it the French pronunciation *oh-zhay*.)

base, bass | Not only homophones, but illogically so. *Base*, as the foot of a pedestal or the corner of a baseball diamond, is phonetically regular. But

bass with a long *a*, meaning low on the musical scale, is a phonetic outlaw. The *a* should be short, as in *bass*, the fish.

bridle path, bridal path | A *bridle path* is a path down which equestrians ride. A *bridal path* is the aisle leading to the altar. Easily confused as a result of either ignorance or experience.

capital, capitol | *Capital* has many meanings, the *Capitol* but one. The latter is the building in which the sessions of the legislature are held. Tie the *o* in *capitol* to the *o* in *dome*. You are probably right to call the hill on which the U.S. Capitol stands Capitol Hill. Nevertheless, Washington, D.C., is the capital city.

cite, site, sight | To *cite* is to call attention to. You *cite* a reference. A police *citation* calls the court's attention to a misdemeanor. A *site* is a place— where a battle was fought or a dam will be built— in fact, the location of anything. All else is *sight*.

complement, compliment | The noun *complement* means a completed quota, as in *the bus had a full complement of passengers*. It also refers to the amount needed to achieve a full quota, as the *complement of an angle* (the angle to be added to make a full right angle). A *compliment* is a laudatory remark.

consensus, census | A *consensus* is an agreement in opinion. To say *consensus of opinion* is redundant. A *census* is an official count, as of the population. The *con-* of *consensus* is often mistaken for a prefix to *census*, resulting in the misspelling *concensus*.

egoism, egotism | Both have to do with *self*, but the first means *an excessive concern with one's interest*, while the second means an *exaggerated opinion of oneself*, that is, conceit.

gourmand, gourmet | The *gourmand* eats too much and too lustily. The *gourmet* makes a fetish of what he eats. Both are a bit of a bore.

input, output | Today we can have on our desktop, computers with more power and convenience than were available ten years ago regardless of size and cost. Along with this revolution in technology have come some changes in English usage. "Software" was a word unknown only thirty years ago, and hardware was what you bought in a hardware store, not at Radio Shack. Along with many new words and images that are needed and obvious are some adaptations I deplore. *Input* and *output* are nouns composed of the prepositions *in* and *out* and the verb *put*. For a century or more these words have stood for (a) the terminals at which signals were introduced, or taken from, a piece of electrical equipment or (b) the signals themselves. Now we encounter such phrases as *the raw data are input over a coaxial*, or *the 16-bit floating point numbers are output on flat strip cable*. So our old noun friends are being used as verbs— what's wrong with that? What's wrong is that the components of these two words keep trying (in my old head) to fly apart and rearrange themselves in proper word order: The raw data are *put in over* a coaxial, and the 16-bit floating point numbers are *put out* (or *delivered*) *over* a flat strip cable. Now

is this a good advance in English? Or is it something to be avoided? What say you?

lama, llama | To quote Ogden Nash:

The one "l" lama is a priest,
The two "l" llama is a beast.
(The three alarmer is a fire.)

lead, led | When it rhymes with *head*, *lead* is the heavy, toxic metal. When it rhymes with *heed*, *lead* is the present tense of the verb whose past tense and past participle is *led*.

lightning, lightening | *Lightning* is the flash that precedes thunder; *lightening* is a decrease in weight or oppressiveness, or a change toward white in paint. Properly pronounced, *light-ning* has two syllables, *light-en-ing* three.

peninsula, peninsular | Both are often misspelled by doubling the first *n*. A *peninsula* is an "almost-island," and the rarely used *peninsular* is the adjective.

principal, principle | *Principal* means *chief* or *foremost* and can be either a noun (a school *principal*) or an adjective (the *principal* cause). A *principle* is a guiding truth or a law of nature and is always a noun.

prophecy, prophesy | The first is a noun meaning *a prediction* and rhymes with *sea*. The second is the verb meaning *to make a prediction* and rhymes with *sigh*. When you *prophesy*, you make a *prophecy*.

Scot, Scotch | Men and women of Scotland prefer to be called *Scots* (or Scotsmen and Scotswomen), but never *Scotch* (or Scotchmen and Scotchwomen). *Scotch* is the whiskey for which Scotland (the land of *Scots*) is famous.

NEVER CONFUSE SCOTCH WHISKEY WITH A SCOT. WOMEN AND MEN OF SCOTLAND PREFER TO BE CALLED SCOTSWOMEN... NEVER SCOTCHWOMEN. DITTO FOR MEN. NEVER SAY SCOTCHMEN.

scull, skull | A *scull* is an oar used for sculling, that is, rowing a boat with the oarlock in the transom and the oar moved from side to side like a fish's tail. A *skull* is what you inhabit (except possibly in moments of madness). Pronounced alike.

silicon, silicone | *Silicon*, pronounced with a short *o* (*-ah-*), is a chemical element. *Silicone*, with a long *o*, is a chemical compound containing *silicon*. *Silicon* is widely used as a substrate and active agent in semiconductor devices such as transistors. California's Santa Clara Valley, where many semiconductor companies are located, has come to be known as Silicon Valley. *Silicones* are quite inert biologically and so have been used for breast implants. Inevitably, some people speak of "Silicone Valley," which is nowhere.

sympathy, empathy | *Sympathy* is a similar reaction or response to a stimulus. *Sympathy* is often exhibited to cheer others in time of sorrow. *Empathy* is the ability to understand how another feels. The Golden Rule is based on *empathy*.

Verbs are the animators of sentences. They make them come alive. It is as if the other parts of speech were merely a cast of characters in a tableau awaiting the touch of the verb to cue them in their roles. Verbs fall into two important classes: **transitive** and **intransitive.**

THE VERB

OTHER PARTS OF SPEECH

VERBS MAKE SENTENCES COME ALIVE

Transitive verbs are the action verbs. They tell what the subject does to the object of the sentence. *Her mother* (the subject) *kept* (the verb) *Mary* (the object) *out of school* (prepositional phrase). The sense of the action passing—or transiting—from subject to object is the basis for the name, which comes from the Latin verb *transere*, to carry over. Further, the object must be explicitly stated for the verb to be called transitive.

Verbs with no object—the intransitive ones—tell us about the actions, state, or condition of the subject. *Harry sat quietly throughout the entire concert. Sat* is intransitive. Failure to distinguish between transitive and intransitive verbs is at the root of many grammatical errors.

English verbs have a comparatively minor amount of inflection, principally to distinguish the past from the present tense but also, in common verbs, to distinguish the person and number. For example, the verb *to be* is conjugated as follows:

Person	Pronoun	Present	Past	Pronoun	Present	Past
	Singular			Plural		
First	I	am	was	we	are	were
Second	you	are	were	you	are	were
Third	he she it	is	was	they	are	were

We note that the inflection of the verb by person is limited to the singular. In regular verbs, it is limited to the present tense and third person singular, where *-s* or *-es* is added: *I climb, you climb, he climbs.* Why this particular inflection should have survived is a bit of a mystery.

The principal parts of a verb are (by convention) the infinitive (minus the *to*), the first person singular past, and the past participle. Thus the principal parts of *be* are *be, was,* and *been.* These parts give an overview of the verb but do not uniquely define its conjugation. They are usually given together in most unabridged dictionaries.

In so-called regular verbs, the past and past participle are formed by adding *-d* or *-ed* to the infinitive form. Thus, *climb, climbed, climbed* is a regular verb. However, there are a great many nearly regular verbs that form their past and past participles by changing the vowel, as in *ring, rang, rung.* Irregular verbs are a hardship for anyone learning a new language. Fortunately, most of you learned to abuse English as your native tongue, so we will not take the space to list the irregular verbs here.

You will note that we have spoken of only two tenses in English, past and present. These are, in fact, the only two that are formed without auxiliary verbs and involve change in the form of the verb itself. All the rest employ auxiliary verbs in combination with the past or present participle of the verb. The following examples illustrate the variety of **time relationships** that can be expressed in this way:

Tense	
Past perfect	I *had gone* when she arrived.
Present perfect	I *have gone* many times.
Past	I often *went.*
Present	I *go* once a month.
Future	I *will go.*
Future Perfect	I *will have gone* by then.

Then there are the so-called **progressive** tenses, which use the present participle of the verb. In the same order, these are:

Tense	
Past perfect	I *had been going.*
Present perfect	I *have been going.*
Past	I *was going.*
Present	I *am going.*
Future	I *will be going.*
Future Perfect	I *will have been going.*

The meaning of these tenses seems intuitive to many of us, but they are very difficult for immigrants whose mother tongue may not have them. All this is neat and tidy, but I haven't included the tense we really use. Let's face it. We never say, *I will go,* just like that. We say, *I'm gonna go.* No wonder there are emigrants as well as immigrants!

Split Infinitives

A **split infinitive** is one in which an adverb—or even a phrase—has been inserted between the *to* and the body of the verb. *To fully understand the situation . . .* is a split infinitive. *To be fully informed about the situation . . .* is not. For decades, even for centuries, students have been enjoined by their mentors not to split infinitives and not to end sentences with prepositions. No good reason was given; these were simply two no-no's.

TODAY, THE ATTITUDE ABOUT SPLIT-INFINITIVES HAS SOFTENED A BIT.

Today, the attitude toward split infinitives seems to be softening a bit, but, because that is true of everything in our schools, we can hardly use that as an excuse to change our own behavior.

Every grammatical rule is a restriction. To merit its existence, a rule should have a net positive effect: It should foster clarity, brevity, and flexibility with little or no sacrifice. Further, it should be consistent with other rules. Elsewhere, we are urged to place modifiers as close as we can to the words they modify. Adjectives should come just before their nouns or pronouns, adverbs just before their adjectives or before or after their verbs. If we were to obey this rule, we would *always* split infinitives, for how much closer can an adverb get than essentially *inside* the verb it modifies? Thus, the split-infinitive ban is inconsistent.

The three possible places for adverbs are before the *to*, between *to* and the *verb*, or after the *verb*. By forbidding the middle position, the split-infinitive ban is restrictive. By outlawing what may be the best choice, it does not increase clarity and often reduces it along with flexibility.

Conclusion: The split-infinitive ban is a bad rule.

How could the prejudice against split infinitives have started? It is true that in most languages, the infinitive is a single word. In Latin, *to be* is *esse*. You can't split that. Thus, it is natural to regard the two English words *to* and *be* as fragments of a single verb and to resist their further separation as one would resist separating a word from its prefix. All plausible, but I expect the truth was that the classic scholars attempted to impose on the upstart English language all the restrictions that were necessary for Latin. "Split infinitives, will they?" I can hear them cry, "We'll jolly well fix their wagon, we'll ban it!"

Whether the classicists actually banned the split infinitive out of spite is debatable but immaterial. The fact is they failed to hail the split infinitive as an asset of this upstart, uninflected language. Had they done so, centuries of English students would have found them prescribed, not proscribed, and would by now have saved the tons of glue needed to cement them back together.

And now a word of caution: Let's not carry this splitting too far. Let's keep the *to* and the *verb* in sight of each other. No circus splits, please.

Moods or Modes

Webster gives the pronunciation that rhymes with *food*, but Fowler says: "It may save misconceptions to mention that the grammar word has nothing to do with the native word meaning *frame of mind*. It is merely a variant of *mode*; that is, any one of the groups of forms in the conjugation of a verb that serve to show the mode or manner by which the action denoted by the verb is represented—*indicative, imperative,* and *subjunctive.*"

Well, then, to avoid further confusion, should we not say what we mean? What is wrong with indicative mode? Imperative mode? Subjunctive mode? All rhyming with *mowed*. I must confess these fall happily on the ear, especially in my analytic mood, and I shall use them.

Almost all English usage is in the **indicative** mode, and though occasional problems arise, they are the common and diverse ones of speaking correctly. The mode itself needs no special comment.

The **imperative** mode is the language of commands.

"GET THEE TO A NUNNERY!"

Get thee to a nunnery. *Go* to the head of the class. *Hold* your horses! *Don't* let it be forgot. The imperative is confined to the second person and consists of omitting the pronoun or inverting its order with the verb. The imperative mode is alive and well, and needs no restoration at this time.

The **subjunctive** mode, on the other hand, seems headed for oblivion. In my opinion, this would be a terrible shame, since the mode confers brevity and clarity as well as a grace and beauty sadly lacking in today's utterances. The **present subjunctive** mode allows us to convey uncertainty in an exquisitely succinct manner. All we need do is use the verb form *be* in place of *is* or *are: If all this be true . . .* does not assert that it is or is not true, but merely allows us to explore the consequences of it's being true. *Be it ever so humble, there's no place like home.* (Home may be a mansion.)

The poet Lowell asks:

> *Oh what is so rare as a day in June?*
> *Then, if ever, come perfect days.*
> *Then heaven tries earth, if it be in tune*
> *And over it softly her warm ear lays.*

We don't really need the subjunctive. We could say: *Then heaven tries earth to see if it is in tune or not.* But somehow it doesn't seem to have the same class. Yet that's where we'll be in a few years unless we resume teaching the niceties of our language.

The **past subjunctive** is used to introduce statements contrary to fact: *"If you were the only girl in the world, and I were the only boy . . . ,"* *"If wishes were horses . . . ,"* and, as Tevye laments, *"If I were a rich man . . ."*

All these are fervent wishes, and that leads some grammarians to say the subjunctive is used in statements expressing a wish. That fact is totally irrelevant. What counts is that the things wished for are contrary to fact.

Just as the present subjunctive is expressed by *be* in all persons and in number, so the past subjunctive is expressed by *were* in all persons and in number. What could be simpler? The entire subjunctive conjugation is composed of two words. In other verbs the conjugation is comparably simple. The third person singular present form drops its -*s* or -*es* and the verb becomes uninflected: *It is not important for the job that he have* (not *has*) *an advanced degree.*

Alan J. Lerner of the American musical theater team of Lerner and Loewe has given us many beautiful lyrics to match Loewe's music, but he lost almost all his credit with the title of the song "If Ever I Would Leave You" from *Camelot.* Not only did he fail to remind us of the proper subjunctive, but the endless repetition of this awkward construction has further corrupted our speech. "Were Ever I to Leave You" would have been a welcome step ahead, and it scans just as well—perhaps better.

Closely related to the subjunctive are conditional phrases and statements. A common error here is the use of *would have* after the conditional *if,* as in, *If I would have known you were coming, I'd have baked a cake.* Write instead, *If I had known* or, even simpler, *Had I known . . . .* All together now: Had I known you were coming, I'd have baked a cake!

Capricious Nonsense

Who would dream of defining two verbs that exchanged their meanings in the first person? What purpose could it possibly serve? Yet this is the case with the common verbs *shall* and *will.* We are supposed (in the best of British tradition) to state **simple futurity,** that is, what we think will happen, by saying:

I shall	we shall
you will	you will
he will she it	they will

and to convey **determination** by saying:

I will	we will
you shall	you shall
he shall she it	they shall

Perhaps at one time this role reversal was natural. Perhaps proponents of free will were happier with *I will* to express determination than *I shall*. Whatever reasons ever existed seem hardly valid today. The continuing confusion caused by the formal rule has blurred the meaning of both words. I urge that we end this nonsense now. Let us use *will* to express futurity in all persons and *shall* to express resolve or determination. This is consistent with the use of *shall* in specifications, where the word denotes a necessary requirement.

The vendor *shall* furnish the necessary tools for . . .

While we are about it, let us straighten out *would* and *should* as well. Let us use *would* to express conditional futurity (*we would if we could*) in all persons, and *should* to represent an implied obligation.

I really believe that rules such as we are seeking to eliminate do more harm than good. They unnecessarily complicate a subject and, by failing to convince students of their worth, lose their interest and allegiance.

Some Problem Verbs

Several pairs of words with closely related meanings are often misused. We will give here their correct usage and our analysis of why the problem exists. If you master these few pages, you will probably cut your grammatical errors in half!

adapt, adopt | To *adapt* is to change so as to be better suited to your purposes. Organisms *adapt* (themselves) to their environment. To *adopt* means to select something as is. You *adopt* a child (you may *adapt* him later). Shall we *adapt* the Constitution to present-day needs, or *adopt* the words of the founders?

affect, effect | *Affect* is a verb meaning to influence, act upon, alter, or modify. (Sometimes it is used to mean pretend, assume, or adopt, but these usages are distinct from those in which there is confusion.) *Effect*, as a noun, means any change or alteration ascribable to a known or assumed cause. Basic fact: When A *affects* B, it produces an *effect*. A mild complication is that *effect* can also be a verb meaning to *bring about*. Notice that in the following examples, the meanings (in parentheses) can be substituted for the correct word used in each example:

> Will the new information *affect* (influence) their opinion?
>
> Can you see any *effect* on (change in) the tissue from the radiation?
>
> Will this legislation *effect* (bring about) significant improvement in public education?
>
> Or will it not *affect* it at all?

aggravate, irritate | To *aggravate* means to worsen, to *add gravity* to a situation, to make a heavy matter heavier. To *irritate* means to annoy, to arouse one's *ire*. Think of this: While the diet may *irritate* you, going off it will surely *aggravate* the problem.

anticipate, expect | To *expect* something means to consider it likely to happen. To *anticipate* means to do something earlier than normal, or before something expected happens, as: *We anticipated the flood by piling sandbags along the bank.* You couldn't *expect* a flood that way. The two words are not synonyms, but *anticipate* is being used as a synonym for *expect* today. We think this is because *anticipate* has four syllables, and *expect* has only two. This gives the sales manager twice as long to decide what his forecast really means. Besides, *anticipate* implies that you have analyzed the

matter and come to these (important) conclusions. Anyone can merely *expect*. In short, *anticipate* has become a pretentious vogue word replacing a humbler word having exactly the right meaning. It is in no better taste to put on airs in writing than in normal conversation.

appraise, apprise | To *appraise* is to estimate the quality of anything from a work of art to a used car. The result is an *appraisal*, which is usually stated in dollars but may read, "Your child needs to improve." To *apprise* is simply to inform. It is the word you want when you shouldn't say *appraise*.

assure, ensure, insure | To *assure* is to build another's confidence, as to *assure* children that there are no monsters under the bed. Then they will *rest assured*. To *ensure* is to make an outcome certain, as to fill the gas tank to *ensure* a nonstop trip. You can *ensure* that . . . , or *assure* yourself that (reflexive). To *insure* means to compensate for a loss by paying the equivalent or appraised worth of the missing (or destroyed) item.

avenge, revenge | Both mean to punish for an earlier injury. You *avenge* another's injury, but you *revenge* your own.

born, borne | Only babies can be *born*, but any load can be *borne*. As any mother will tell you, what is *born* must be *borne* for a long time. Probably this connection led to the homophone, which must be distinguished by its spelling.

cannon, canon | A *cannon* is an early large gun with an unrifled barrel that shoots balls rather than cylindrical loads. A *canon* is a standard of good taste or judgment. The church has no *cannons* but plenty of *canons*. A *canon* can also be a contrapuntal musical composition.

censor, censure | To *censor* is to delete and suppress material for reasons of morality or national security. A *censor* (noun) does this tricky job. To *censure* is to criticize harshly, to reprimand officially.

damp, dampen | As engineering students, we were warned never to confuse *damp*, whose meaning is to choke, stifle, or cause to diminish, with *dampen*, whose primary meaning is to moisten or wet. The butterfly valve in a stovepipe, which you use to reduce the draft and thereby lessen the heat, is a *damper*, not a *dampener*. When you suppressed a parasitic oscillation in a circuit, you *damped*, not *dampened*, it. Shock absorbers do not "absorb shocks," but they *damp*, not *dampen*, the bouncing of your car's suspension. I have always found the distinction useful, but there is a growing tendency to ignore it. Perhaps the term *wet blanket*, which both *damps* your enthusiasm and *dampens* you, is the culprit. Ignore the distinction at your peril. You may end up singing, *"but I'm just mean enough to slap your dampener down,"* which is not what you really intended.

exercise, exorcise | In some circles, *exercise* is considered the cure-all for physical ailments. While *exercising* gains adherents every day, *exorcism* is a dying art, there being so few ghosts available today.

forego, forgo | *Forego* means simply to precede: *to go before*. *Forgo* means to give something up, *to do without*.

imply, infer | To *imply* is to suggest something indirectly, rather than by a forthright statement. If you, as a speaker, are successful with your *implications*, your listeners will draw the correct *inferences*. That is, they will *infer* what you intended. The writer or speaker *implies*, the reader or listener *infers*.

HENS LAY EGGS. SO DO COMEDIANS. THIS CAN CONFUSE THE USE OF LIE AND LAY.

lay, lie | Misuse of these two verbs accounts for a substantial fraction of grammatical errors. If not the number one solecism, it certainly belongs in the top ten. I don't know what educational technique, if any, is to blame, but something didn't click. Often, if I say, "That word should be *lie*," the young man will blink and exclaim, "Oh, of course! Hens *lay* eggs!" as if he had suddenly remembered a relevant law of nature. Well, comedians *lay* eggs, too. But what either of these physiologically different but grammatically correct acts have to do with the correct use of *lay* or *lie* is beyond me.

At this point, all I should need to tell you is that *lay* is a transitive verb, with principal parts *lay, laid, laid,* while *lie* is intransitive, with principal parts *lie, lay, lain,* and let you mend your own ways, if necessary. But I suspect this is all a little new, and you may appreciate a helping hand.

Lay means to put something down: *Pistol-packin' mama, lay that pistol down!* Being transitive, *lay* must take an object, and, conversely, if there is an object, *lay's* the word. *Lie* means to assume a reclining position:

I think I'll lie down for a nap. But, *Now I lay me* (the object) *down to sleep.* The correct forms for *lay* are:

> I *lay* the book on the table.
> Yesterday, I *laid* the book on the table.
> I have *laid* the book there every day this year.

Book is the **object** in all these examples.

For *lie* we have:

> The book *lies* (or *is lying*) on the table.
> The book *lay* (or *was lying*) on the table yesterday.
> The book *has lain* on the table for days.

Book is the **subject** in all these examples.

Probably the confusion began because the past tense of *lie* is, of all things, *lay.* But we should be able to live with that. More important, I suspect, was the catapulting into colloquial use of the word *lay,* meaning either the object of (noun) or the commission of (verb) sexual intercourse. Since an alternate meaning of *lie* is to tell falsehoods, and since *laying* involved two people *lying* (often in both senses) you can see that our present confusion was inevitable.

The solution is obvious. *Lie* quietly in the sun and decide what you want to be: a *layer,* a *lier,* a *liar,* or a *lexicographer*—a compiler of a dictionary, defined by Samuel Johnson as "a shameless drudge who busies himself in tracing the origin, and detailing the significant application of words."

misuse, abuse | To *misuse* means to use for the wrong purpose or in a wrong way. To *abuse* means to *misuse* in such a way as to cause damage, or to hurt physically or psychically. Words are *misused*; language is *abused*. *Abuse* also implies intent.

overlook, oversee | To *overlook* can mean to have a commanding view, as in: *The castle overlooks the entire valley*. Paradoxically, it can also mean to fail to see or to disregard. To *oversee* is to manage or supervise.

pore, pour | The verb *pore*, usually followed by *over*, means to study something intently or to think deeply about an issue until it is time to *pour* a drink. In this sense, the two are mutually exclusive.

pray, prey | To *pray* means to enter a plea for, as to *pray* for lenience (or even for justice) in a court or to ask for a suspension of natural law by some deity. To *prey* is to hunt for, or make a victim of, especially for food, as in: *Cats prey on mice*. Also, figuratively it means to distress, as in: *To prey on one's mind*.

prescribe, proscribe | One letter makes these two opposites. The doctor *prescribes* (albeit illegibly) the medicine he thinks you need and *proscribes* foods you should *not* eat.

raise, rise | *Raise* is a transitive verb meaning to elevate. Its principal parts are *raise, raised, raised*. It must have an object: you *raise* your employees' pay, the roof, and your kids. *Rise* is always intransitive and means to stand up, to ascend. Its principal parts are *rise, rose, risen*. It never takes an object. You *rise* to speak, to the occasion, and (sometimes) above your principles. Children *raise* a fuss. The dough *rises*. So do prices. Both words can be nouns. Inflation causes a *rise* in prices, which forces *raises* in pay. Is there a problem here? Yes, but it's not grammatical.

ravage, ravish | To *ravage* is to damage severely: *The tornadoes ravaged the little town*. *Ravish* is a pleasure-pain word that implies violence in lust. Use with caution. Not every girl who wishes to look *ravishing* wants to be *ravished*.

rotate, revolve | To *rotate* means to turn on an axis. The earth *rotates* once a (sidereal) day. To *revolve* means to move on a closed path, called the orbit, around some other object or point. The earth's *rotation* makes the day, its *revolution* about the sun makes the year. That's how astronomers distinguish the two. Nevertheless, your tachometer reads *revolutions* per minute. Ah me.

set, sit, seat | *Set (set, set, set)* is transitive in the sense of *put in place* or *adjust*, intransitive in the sense of *congeal* or *stiffen*, as a glue. *Sit (sit, sat, sat)* is always intransitive and means to assume or be in an upright position, as in a chair. There need never be confusion between these words. As a matter of fact, the exceptions that do exist are a legacy from days of innocence. The *setting* of the sun is an idiom that stresses the sun's slow apparent descent (its *settling*) more than its repose on anything in the west. We do not visualize this million-mile-diameter ball of fire *sitting* on anything. At the other extreme, a *setting* hen is really *sitting* as hard as she can, but farmers have used the wrong word for so long they've got us doing it. Anybody care?

As a transitive verb, *seat (seat, seated, seated)* means to *install in office* or, in more modest situations, simply to *provide with a seat*. This is the word you want, dear hostess, when you are trying not to say, *"I'm going to sit you over there."* Neither *sit* nor *set* will do. *Seat's* the word.

shone, shined | Both are the past term and past participles of *shine*. For *shine* in the sense of glow, use *shone*. For *shine* in the sense of polish, use *shined*. *His shoes were shined until they shone.*

smelled, smelt | Either will do as the past and past participle of *smell*, but the former is preferred to avoid confusion with the *smelting* of ores and also the little fish.

stammer, stutter | Both are speech difficulties. The former is preferred when the symptom is involuntary and repeated hesitation, the latter when the problem is staccato repetition of consonants, especially initial consonants.

Adjectives and adverbs are the spice of our speech. Both modify (that is, describe and qualify) the words they act on, thereby adding color and depth to our prose. Adjectives modify nouns and pronouns, giving what we might call mini-descriptions of their subjects. It was not any house; it was a *big, white, rambling* house. Adverbs modify verbs and thereby provide additional information about the action. Heads! I cried *frantically,* before the coin landed. In the examples above, *big, white,* and *rambling* all modify the noun *house,* so are adjectives, while *frantically* modifies the verb *cried,* so is an adverb. Adverbs also modify adjectives and other adverbs.

Many adjectives can be converted to adverbs merely by adding -*ly* (*clear/clearly, eager/eagerly*) or by dropping -*y* and adding -*ily* (*happy/happily*), but it would be a mistake to conclude that all adverbs end in -*ly.* They don't and, what's more, many adjectives do! We speak of the *daily* paper, *elderly* people, a *lovely* evening, a *lively* dance, a *kindly* gentleman, and an *early* bird, to name a few. All modify nouns and so are adjectives. Many words can be either adjectives or adverbs:

We say	And we also say
a fast train	He ran fast.
a tight skirt	Hold tight!
a straight road	Go straight on.
a long journey	He worked long and hard.
a hard choice	He worked hard at his new job.
a low blow	Swing low, sweet chariot.

Of course, the highway signs GO SLOW and DRIVE SLOW have taken their toll, making an adverb of *slow,* but don't get carried away. Editors will still expect you to write *slowly* and *carefully.* Well, *carefully* anyway.

There is also a "macho" school that seems to regard adverbs as a dainty affectation and that substitutes adjectives everywhere. *That was real nice of you, lady,* they say, or *we had a little trouble with this filly at first, but lately she rides real good.* These types are to be found in western movies, cigarette ads, and pool halls. They need not concern us here.

There is an opposite tendency, in technical or expository papers, to list the reasons for or against the subject and to introduce them with the words *firstly, secondly, thirdly. . . .* We might call this a "tabular" construction, used by the writer in lieu of a more formal table. But why the *-ly* endings?

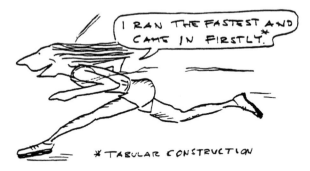

I RAN THE FASTEST AND CAME IN FIRSTLY.*

* TABULAR CONSTRUCTION

If the list were long, should we expect to encounter *seventhly* and *thirteenthly*? Two comments are relevant: The ordinal numbers (first, second, third, and so on) belong to the class that are either adjectives or adverbs, so there is no need to add *-ly.* But perhaps more important (not importantly), where is the verb that these supposed adverbs are modifying? It seems natural to me to regard *first* as an abbreviation for *in the first place,* and so on. So let us relax and write simply *first . . ., second . . .,* and *third.* Otherwise, we may end up with directions for making rabbit stew that begin, "Firstly, catch a rabbit."

Strunk and White,[4] in speaking about words like *over, much,* and *first,* say: "Do not dress up words by adding *-ly* to them, as though putting a hat on a horse."

Comparison of Adjectives and Adverbs

Comparison is the word used to describe the changes in form of modifiers (or the use of auxiliary words) to indicate the relative degree of the **quality** possessed by the subject word. Sue is a *pretty* girl, but Linda is *prettier,* and Cynthia is *prettiest.* The degrees of comparison are **positive** (for *pretty*), **comparative** (for *prettier*), and **superlative** (for *prettiest*).

Most adjectives and adverbs of one syllable form their comparatives by adding *-er* and their superlative by adding *-est* to the positive form. When this would cause pronunciation problems, we use the positive form and add *more* for the comparative and *most* for the superlative. Thus we have:

Positive	Comparative	Superlative
eager	more eager	most eager
happy	happier	happiest
slow	slower	slowest
rapidly	more rapidly	most rapidly
rapidly	less rapidly	least rapidly

As the last example shows, "downward" comparison to a smaller and the smallest extent of the modifier uses the words *less* and *least* instead of *more* and *most*. We also note that the superlative does not always mean the *best* or *most* but simply the *extreme* of whatever quality the modifier confers.

The modifiers of **quantity** are the auxiliary words we have been using. Their own comparisons are:

much	more	most
little	less	least

The modifiers of **number** are:

many	more	most
few	fewer	fewest

We note that the modifiers of quantity and number coincide in the comparative *more* and the superlative *most*, but elsewhere they are distinct. A very common error is to use the modifier of quantity when the modifier of number is called for. We frequently hear *less* people rather than *fewer* people, so frequently, in fact, that it may not even disturb the ear. It may be less noticeable, but is no less egregious than to say *many* water. The correct forms are *more* water and *fewer* people. (California politicians take note.)

Formal English permits the superlative only when three or more examples are being compared. It's like the prepositions *between* and *among*. To be *among* alternatives, there must be three or more, while for only two you are *between* them. You can be the *prettiest* of five candidates, but only the *prettier* of two.

Finally, we note that some modifiers do not admit comparison in that the condition or quality itself has no degree but is either there fully or not at all. Examples are *unique, perfect,* and *pregnant*.

Something is either the only one in existence or it is not. Nothing can be *more* unique or *most* unique. Pregnancy is also considered to be all or nothing, although many women would argue that they were really *more* pregnant at nine months than at nine minutes!

Predicate Adjectives and Verbs of Perception

The **predicate** is the verb and the part of a sentence that occurs after the verb. The verb itself is sometimes called the immediate predicate. When we say, *This book is dull*, or *My uncle is becoming senile*, the words *dull* and *senile* are called predicate adjectives. That is, they occur after the verb (*is* or *is becoming*) and modify the subject of the verb (*book* or *uncle*). In olden days, the verb that tied the subject and a predicate adjective together was called a *copula*, from the Latin *copulere*, to couple or join. Some common **copulas** are:

be	grow
become	remain
seem	stay

As you can imagine, that name didn't last long in our public schools and was quickly replaced with the term *linking* verb. This helped to keep order in the classroom, but didn't clarify the grammar much, since all verbs link something to something else.

However, let us accept the term, since the one important thing to realize is that, as a result of the verb, the modifier operates on the subject of the sentence (a noun or pronoun) and is therefore an adjective, never an adverb.

Predicate adjectives are commonly found in connection with the verbs of **perception**:

appear	smell
feel	sound
look	taste

Thus, in the examples below, the words *easy, sad, good, sweet, fine,* and *sour* are all predicate adjectives.

> The problem appears *easy.*
> That news makes me feel *sad.*
> That dress looks *good* on you.
> The flowers smell *sweet.*
> The stereo sounds *fine* to me.
> The milk tastes *sour.*

Sometimes homonyms confuse the use of an adjective-adverb pair. The classic case is that of *good* and *well. Good* is an adjective meaning possessed of desirable qualities, and *well* is the adverb. It was a *good* play and *well* acted. But *well* is also an adjective meaning in a state of good health. You can look *good* (predicate adjective) because you are *well* or, in short, you can look *well.* But a dress cannot look *well.* It can look *good* (predicate adjective) on you but not *well* on you.

What about expressions like *Good going!* Is *good* modifying a verb? It looks that way, but actually the present participle *going* is really a gerund in this idiom, that is, a verb form used as a noun. Saved by the bell!

Notice that the linking verbs are all intransitive, though they may not appear so at first glance.

We have called adverbs and adjectives the spice of prose. We should add that too much spice can spoil the writing just as fast as it can spoil the dish. The prime effort should be to pick the right words in the first place. As E.B. White says: "Write with [the proper] nouns and verbs, not with adjectives and adverbs. The adjective hasn't been built that can pull a weak or inaccurate noun out of a tight place . . . [Avoid qualifiers] like *rather, very, little, pretty* . . . we should all try to do a *little* better, we should be *very* watchful of this rule, for it is a *rather* important one, and we are *pretty* sure to violate it now and then." Good

advice, but it is taking us beyond the scope of this little book, out of the shallows of simple grammatical error and into the treacherous high seas of style.

Misused Modifiers

As with the other parts of speech, there are certain pairs of adjectives and adverbs that tend to be confused. Some examples follow:

all together, altogether | The first means that all are in the same place or doing something at the same time. *Altogether* means in total, the sum of all effects.

alternate, alternative | *Alternate* requires two *alternatives*, no more, no less. Then it means that the *alternatives* take turns, first A, then B, then A again. Then and only then will the *alternatives* alternate.

anxious, eager | We have become so accustomed to saying, I'm *anxious* to know the outcome, that we seldom hear a different word. I *anxiously* await your reply. Really? Are you worried and sleepless? Do you pace the floor? If not, isn't it possible that you are merely *eager*? I eagerly await your reply.

aural, oral, verbal | The two homophones refer to the ears and the mouth respectively. *Oral* also means given by mouth as an oral medication or an oral examination. *Verbal* means related to words. A verbal examination could be written and used to test your vocabulary, for example.

backward, backwards | Only the first can be used as an adjective: a *backward* glance. Either can be used as an adverb. Try it and see.

bad, badly | These two modifiers, which give little trouble ordinarily, are often confused in the expression: *I feel bad. Bad* here is a predicate adjective. The only use for which *I feel badly* could be considered grammatically is if it were spoken by a blind man who is making many mistakes reading his Braille messages.

beside, besides | *Beside* means at the side of: And thou *beside* me in the wilderness. . . . *Besides* means in addition to. What is there to eat *besides* the roast?

blond, blonde | One of our few words with gender. Men are blond (as are races), women are blondes.

BLOND   BLONDE

cardinal, ordinal | The *cardinal* numbers are those we count with: one, two, three, etc. The *ordinal* numbers define the position of the referent in a series. If something is seventh, six other events have gone before and others may follow. Ordinal numbers are often construed by writers as adverbs and meaninglessly adorned with *-ly* endings.

climatic, climactic, climacteric | The first pertains to climate and the weather, the second to climaxes, as in a play. The seldom-used noun *climacteric* refers to a moment in life or history when significant changes have been brought about, the watershed between eras (with or without bloodshed). The Cuban missile crisis was also a *climacteric* in U.S.-Russian relations.

contagious, infectious | *Contagious* means apt to be spread by contact between infected persons. *Infectious* means spread by the mobility of the microorganisms themselves.

continual, continuous, constant | *Continual* means happening often but with possible interruptions. *Continuous* means without interruption, and *constant* means without any change at all.

credible, credulous | *Credible* means believable, *incredible* means unbelievable. *Credulous* means inclined to believe, *incredulous* means difficult to convince. The subject matter is *credible* or *incredible,* the listener *credulous* or *incredulous.*

discreet, discrete | *Discreet* means careful and considerate, reserved in behavior. *Discrete* means occurring in distinct pieces as opposed to continuous.

discriminating, discriminatory | A *discriminating* person shows judgment and discernment in differentiating among options. A *discriminatory* person is one who is unfair, biased, or prejudiced. There's no harm in discriminating—just do it for the right reasons.

eminent, imminent | *Eminent* means well known or distinguished, and refers only to persons. *Imminent* means about to happen, impending. It is rarely used in referring to persons.

especially, specially, specifically | *Especially* means exceptionally, to a high degree, as in: This lotion is *especially* effective for hives. *Specially* means for a particular purpose: These planes were *specially* designed for high accelerations. *Specifically* is used to denote a particular case: A few drugs and, *specifically*, cocaine were once thought to be harmless.

famous, notorious, infamous | All mean widely known; the question is, for what? Lincoln is *famous*, Evil Knievil *notorious*, and Hitler *infamous*.

farther, further | The first and only the first should be used for real distances: Chicago is *farther* from San Francisco than from New York. The second and only the second should be used for figurative distances: Upon looking *further* into the matter, or Nothing could be *further* from my mind.

forceful, forcible, forced | In spite of Will Strunk's[4] preference for *forcible*, the other two have their places. *Forceful* means full of force, as in a *forceful* argument or *forceful* presentation. *Forcible* means accomplished by force, as in a *forcible* entry. *Forced* implies either inevitability, as in a *forced* conclusion or obtained by force, as a *forced* confession.

healthy, healthful | *Healthy* means full of good health, robust. One can also speak of a *healthy* appetite, meaning one that is alive and well and hard to suppress. One can also idiomatically speak of taking a *healthy* swing at a ball. But one should not call foods *healthy*, for they can merely confer good health upon the consumer. The proper word is *healthful*.

inflammable, flammable | Both words have the same meaning: easily ignited. Let us eschew the former and thereby avoid the mistake of interpreting the prefix *in-* as meaning *not* instead of *into*.

INGENIOUS FINANCIER   INGENUOUS INVESTOR

ingenious, ingenuous | An *ingenious* person is clever, resourceful, inventive, a near genius. An *ingenuous* person is simple and trusting, guileless.

intolerant, intolerable | A matter of viewpoint. The *intolerant* person finds life (and others) *intolerable*.

less, fewer | Use less for quantity, *fewer* for number. See modifiers of number, page 35.

melted, molten | *Melted* is used for substances such as ice cream or butter that become liquid near or below room temperature. *Molten* is used for substances like glass, lead, or iron that become liquid only at high temperatures. It takes a furnace to make something *molten*, a refrigerator to keep other things from *melting*.

noisy, noisome | *Noisy* things offend the ear; *noisome* things offend the nose or are in some way disgusting.

peremptory, perfunctory | A *peremptory* manner is imperious, dogmatic, or decisive. A *peremptory* matter is urgent, compelling, and may *preempt*

(notice the spelling difference) the attention of the directors. *Perfunctory* means routine, cursory, as a *perfunctory* glance.

soluble, solvable | *Soluble* means easily dissolved, usually in water. Either is used to mean capable of being solved, but I prefer the latter as being less ambiguous.

strait, straight | *Strait* means narrow, confining, as in the *Straits of Gibraltar* or a *straitjacket*. *Straight* is the antonym (opposite) of *crooked*.

suspicious, suspect | To be *suspicious* means to be distrustful of another. The related word *suspicion* is a noun—you can have a *suspicion*—but it is never a verb. You cannot *suspicion* someone, you *sus-SPECT* him. *SUS-pect* is the noun. If you act in a *suspicious* manner, you can become a *SUS-pect*.

transparent, translucent | A glass window is *transparent*, and a bathroom window is often *translucent*. *Translucent* objects let light through, but disperse it so no images can be seen.

valuable, valued, valueless, invaluable, priceless | *Valuable* means having value—especially market value. *Valued* means treasured, irrespective of the market. *Valueless* means of no value, the opposite of the first two. *Invaluable* does not mean valueless; it means of great value or highly valued. *Priceless* is not a synonym of *valueless*, either. On the contrary, it means so *valuable* that any price would be meaningless. Got that all straight?

owhere is our grammatical ignorance more evident than in the daily deluge of misused pronouns. Speakers unable to decide between *I* and *me* opt for *myself,* apparently in the mistaken belief that it would be right in either case. As a

matter of fact, *myself* is seldom a proper substitute for *I* or *me*, and its use further reveals the speaker's ignorance. To cure your pronoun problems requires a rudimentary knowledge of grammar and a rehearsal of the correct forms until they spring automatically to the lips with no conscious reasoning. I can't help you rehearse, but I can get you started with the needed grammar concepts. So be my pupil for an hour. There's nothing on TV anyway!

A Little Grammar for Thine Own Sake

The **subject** of a sentence is the part being talked about. It is usually a noun or pronoun that occurs before the verb. A *compound subject* consists of more than one person or thing. The *predicate* is what is said about the *subject*. It is usually the rest of a simple sentence. Example:

Harry and I	*went for a hike.*
Subject	Predicate
(Compound)	(Prepositional Phrase)

Pronouns take the place of nouns in speech and writing. This is done for brevity and to avoid repetition. But whereas nouns are essentially uninflected (do not change their form) in English, pronouns (especially personal pronouns) have retained a considerable amount of inflection. There are many kinds of pronouns: personal, reflexive-intensive, relative, interrogative, restrictive and nonrestrictive, as well as definite and indefinite. We will have a few words to say about each, but it is the personal pronouns and their declension (systematic order) that bring out the worst in us, so let us begin there.

In English, as in almost any language, there are three **persons**:

Person	
First person	the speaker or writer
Second person	the person or group addressed
Third person	anyone or anything else

Then there are three English **cases**:

Case	
Nominative	the case of the subject of the sentence, the one named
Objective	the case of the objects of verbs or prepositions
Possessive	the case indicating ownership

There is also **number**: singular and plural.

And finally, there is **gender**: masculine, feminine, and neuter.

In a highly inflected language, all combinations would be distinct, thus requiring 3 x 3 x 2 x 3 or 54 personal pronouns. But because in English gender inflects only the *third person singular*, we need fewer than half that number. In addition, the *second person* tends to be uninflected. The actual **personal pronouns** are:

Person	Singular	Plural	Case
1	I	we	
2	you	you	Nominative
3	he she it	they	
1	me	us	
2	you	you	Objective
3	him her it	them	
1	my (mine)	our (ours)	
2	your (yours)	your (yours)	Possessive
3	his (his) her (hers) its (its)	their (theirs)	

Notice that in the possessive case, two forms of the pronoun are given. The first, without parentheses, is the "adjectival" form, used when the noun of the possessed object is stated, as in *my car* or *her towel*. The second is the "stand-alone" form, also called the absolute form, as in *this car is mine*, or *this towel is hers*. I am not aware of many problems with possessive pronouns, so let us confine our attention to the first two cases. There we notice that the second person is uninflected and that in the third person *it* is also uninflected. That leaves us with only ten pronouns to worry about. Since there is never any doubt as to which person you are using or whether the singular or plural is needed, the whole problem boils down to knowing which case you are in. Finally, if we agree that you can easily recognize the possessive case, the single decision to be made is whether the pronoun is in the nominative or objective case. So here is the problem in a nutshell:

Nominative	Objective
I	me
he	him
she	her
we	us
they	them

Which column do we pick our pronoun(s) from?

RULE #1
The subject of a verb and all pronouns referring to the subject (predicate nominatives) are in the nominative case.

> **They are a boisterous group.**
> (*They* is the subject *of are.*)
>
> **He and I are longtime friends.**
> (*He* and *I* are the compound subject of *are.*)
>
> **Could that already be they at the door?**
> (*They* refers to the subject of *be.*)
>
> **It might have been she.**
> (But it had to be *you.*)

Since most of us easily recognize the subject of a sentence, these "up-front" pronouns are apt to be correct. More frequent is our failure to use the nominative case for predicate nominatives. For the present, until practice makes them evident, it is convenient to expect a predicate nominative following some form of the verb *to be* (*am, is, are, may have been,* etc.). See the above examples. The shortest predicate nominative on record is the answer to *Who goes there?* Properly, the answer is:

It is I. But we have used the wrong form for so long that the correct form sounds odd. The French do it, too. They say *C'est moi,* or *It is me.*

This makes all of us proper subjects for testing the efficacy of rehearsal. Go around saying *It is I* to yourself a hundred times a day for a week. Chances are you'll use the correct form the rest of your days, such is the power of habituation.

The direct object of a (transitive) verb receives the action of that verb. The indirect object tells for what purpose, or to whom, or for whom the action was done.

> **Give the marbles to your brother.**
> **Give your brother the marbles.**

The marbles are the direct object, *your brother* the indirect. As the examples show, either can come first. There is no need to distinguish the two in

English, since both take the objective case. In pronouns: Give *them* to *him*. (Both objective.) Notice that if the direct object comes first, we need the preposition *to* before the indirect object.

RULE #2
The objects of a verb, direct and indirect, and the object of a preposition are in the objective case.

Prepositions are words that show the spatial or temporal relation of a noun or pronoun to another word in the sentence. Prepositions usually occur in phrases and usually at the beginning. *Across the river* and *under the trees* are prepositional phrases. The nouns at the end are the objects, but because nouns are uninflected in English, they do not display their case. Substitute a pronoun and the case must be objective: *across me* or *under him*.

So too for the list below of common prepositions. They can only be followed by the personal pronouns *me, him, her, us, them*, plus, of course, *you* and *it*:

about	*below*	*for*	*throughout*
above	*beneath*	*from*	*to*
across	*beside*	*in*	*toward*
after	*besides*	*into*	*under*
against	*between*	*like*	*underneath*
along	*beyond*	*of*	*until*
amid	*but*	*off*	*unto*
among	*by*	*on*	*up*
around	*concerning*	*over*	*upon*
at	*down*	*past*	*with*
before	*during*	*since*	*within*
behind	*except*	*through*	*without*

Above us, concerning them, after him, whatever your preposition and pronoun, always, ALWAYS use the objective case. NEVER say: *before we*, or *for I*, or *between you and I*.

With compound subjects and objects, the selection rules are the same for both pronouns, so their cases ALWAYS agree:

> **He and I are both sailors.**
> (Both nominative)
> **This math is beyond John and me.**
> (Both objective; only the pronoun shows it)
> **The mouse ran over me but under him.**
> (Both objective)

This leads to the well-known rule for testing: When in doubt, leave one pronoun out, then the other:

> **Dad gave a shirt to me.**
> (Certainly not to *I!*)
> **Dad gave a shirt to her.**
> (Certainly not to *she!*)

Therefore:

> **Dad gave a shirt to me and her.**
> (Or, *to her and me*, but NOT *to her and I*.)

If the object of a preposition is a noun preceded by a possessive pronoun, the pronoun retains its possessive case. *They recommended a new coat of paint for my* (not *me*) *house*. Closely related to this is the use of the possessive case with many participial phrases:

> **Do you mind *my* (not *me*) interrupting you to ask questions?**

The point is that what you may object to is not *me*, but *my interruptions*.

Double Billing

If you use the noun, don't use the pronoun too as if to be sure you've been heard. Don't say *My uncle he had false teeth*, or *My sister she is engaged*, unless you are describing a character who really talks that way. (In that case, all's fair, if you can handle it!) This is really a special case of what we call unnecessary words. These are discussed on page 60.

Change of Case

Sometimes the same thing is the object of one verb or preposition and the subject of another. Sometimes the change seems to take place while the first person is right in your hand, so to speak:

> Let *him* (not *he*) who cast the stone stand up and take a bow.

Him is the object of the verb *let*, and *who* (not *whom*) is the subject of the verb *cast*. All is well as written in the above example. Do not worry that the objective case of the personal pronoun is cheek-by-jowl with the nominative case of the relative pronoun *who*. The adverbial phrase *who cast the stone* is inserted to clarify which *him* we mean. Without the phrase, the sentence would read: *Let him stand up and take a bow*, which is all right too. You'd never say: *Let he stand up*. Although *he* is the subject of *stand*, *him* is the object of the transitive imperative *let*—a more compelling connection.

Reflexive and Intensive Pronouns

Now that we have resolved how to choose among *I*, *me*, or *my*, it is probably safe to introduce the so-called **reflexive-intensive** pronouns:

myself	ourselves
yourself	yourselves
himself, herself, itself	themselves

In formal English, there are only two proper uses for these types of pronouns. One is in sentences in which the subject and object are the same: *Jane just hurt herself*. This is the **reflexive** use. The action is reflexed, or bent back on itself.

The second use is to provide emphasis: *He did it all himself*, or *He, himself, did all the work*. This is called the intensive use. Note that the *himself* in these examples refers to the pronoun *he*. The reference is necessary, and may also be a (proper) noun, as in: *Charles did all the work himself*, or "I did it all myself," said the Little Red Hen.

Most experts agree that there is no appropriate use for reflexive-intensive pronouns other than those described above.

As Red Smith, the erstwhile sportswriter, once said, referring to sentences like *He invited Mary and myself to dinner,* "*Myself* is the refuge of idiots taught early that *me* is a dirty word." So, unless you are willing to risk nomination to Smith's Hall of Idiocy, you'd better stick to good old *I* or *me,* whichever is the proper case.

Relative Pronouns

These pronouns are used to begin subordinate clauses. They are called relative because they relate to an earlier noun or pronoun called the antecedent. One of the skills of writing is to choose a word order that reveals the antecedent unambiguously. The **relative pronouns** are:

what	who (nominative)
which	whom (objective)
that	whose (possessive)

Examples:

> The *people who* complain most are often **professionals.**
> He is a *man whom* we can trust.
> Do you know the *woman whose* son was hurt?

As the second and third examples show, there is no need for the relative pronoun and its antecedent to agree in case. In the second example, *man* is nominative, *whom* is objective—the object of *trust.* In the last example, *woman* is the object of *know,* and *whose* is possessive.

Restrictive and Nonrestrictive Pronouns

The proper usage of *that* and *which* has been the subject of much contention. Here we will join Fowler[3] and White,[4] who recommend that *that* be used to introduce **restrictive** clauses and that **nonrestrictive** clauses be introduced by *which* and be set off by commas.

A restrictive clause is one that limits or restricts the field of choice by defining some property of the subject:

> The television set *that needs fixing* is in the den.

This means that we have more than one TV set and that only the one in the den needs fixing. *Restrict* your attention to that one.

On the other hand, we might say:

> The television set, *which needs fixing,* is in the den.

By this we mean that our only TV is in the den and, by the way, it needs repair. The clause does not narrow the field—it is nonrestrictive.

This rule may seem a bit complicated at first, but it becomes second nature. It is helpful in that the choice of *that* versus *which* is now information-bearing. Try it. You'll like it.

Definite and Indefinite Pronouns

The **definite** pronouns are *this, that, these,* and *those.* They make clear what the speaker is referring to and are sometimes called **demonstrative** pronouns:

That is my car over there.
This is the road to Boston.
Which are yours, *these* in my hand or *those* over there?

By contrast, we have, finally, the indefinite pronouns that refer to no one or no thing specifically. (Compare these with the articles *a* and *the*.) The **indefinite** pronouns are:

Singular			Either	Plural
another	every	none	all	both
anybody	everybody	no one	any	few
anyone	everyone	one	most	many
each	nobody	somebody	some	several
either	neither	someone	such	none

The column headings indicate whether the subject associated with these pronouns is considered singular or plural or can be either. Thus we have:

No one knows the answer.
All is well.
All of the games were fine.
Many apply, but *few* are chosen.

The most frequent errors are the use of plural forms where the singular is called for, as in:

Will everyone bring *their* checkbook?

Formally, this should be (and formerly was):

Will everybody bring *his* checkbook?

But now, in these days of equal rights, we are encouraged to say his/her, which is impossible. The problem is, of course, that the desire to be politically correct has created a need for *third person singular* personal pronouns that imply masculine *or* feminine but *not* neuter. Actually, we need three (or four) pronouns, one each for the nominative and objective cases and one (or two) for the possessive.

The remaining parts of speech are the conjunctions and interjections. The latter are exclamations or epithets literally thrust into a sentence—as the name implies—and often bear no direct relation to the grammar of the host sentence. They are not a common source of error and therefore need not concern us here. Conjunctions, on the other hand, play an important role in establishing the relation between the words and "substructures" of the sentence and deserve our consideration. Before we can discuss their usage, we must first understand what the substructures are that these conjunctions connect.

Phrases and Clauses

Clarity requires that certain words be close together —that adjectives come immediately before their nouns, adverbs be close to the words they modify, prepositions be near their objects, and so on. Short clusters of closely related words are called **phrases**. These often do the work of a single part of speech, so we have noun phrases, prepositional phrases, verb phrases, etc. Germans go one step further, they actually fuse together the words of a phrase

to form one splendid special word, minted for the occasion. Thus a German might speak of the *Geschwindigkeitsbegrenze* where we would use the phrase *speed limit*. *Speed limit* is a noun phrase, with *limit* being the noun.

The auxiliaries that determine the tenses of English verbs can be considered verb phrases: When you arrive *we will have been long gone*. Notice that this verb phrase is the entire predicate of the sentence.

Prepositional phrases are especially common. They consist of the preposition and its object, which may itself be a noun phrase: *over the fireplace, in the master bedroom, on the back porch* are examples. Here a prepositional phrase is the subject of the sentence: *After the final examination* will be too late.

If phrases are like German "macrowords," **independent** clauses are mini-sentences, for they must contain a subject and a predicate. In fact, there is no internal difference between an independent clause and a *simple* sentence. *Compound* sentences contain two or more independent clauses but no dependent clauses: The dogwood in Yosemite were all in bloom, *and* we drove quite slowly to enjoy the beauty. This is a compound sentence with two independent clauses connected by the conjunction *and.* Finally, a *complex* sentence contains at least one *dependent* clause in addition to one or more *independent* clauses. The relation between independent and dependent (or subordinate) clauses will become clearer when we illustrate the use of the conjunctions that connect them.

Conjunctions

It is not the mere joining together by conjunctions of words, phrases, and clauses that merits study, it is their role in defining the relation of these parts to one another and to the meaning of the sentence. The simplest conjunctions are the **coordinating conjunctions**, exemplified by *and, but, or,* and *nor.*

These do not subordinate one connected entity to the other, but they do call attention to different aspects of the relation: *And* emphasizes the similarities and implies that statements made apply to

NERVOUS STUDENT UNKNOWINGLY STAMMERS THE COORDINATING CONJUNCTIONS

either or both. *And* in grammar is like the inclusive *or* of logic. *But* is used to introduce exceptions to the first entity, as in: We tried every way *but* the right way. *But* can also introduce a compensating thought: a sadder *but* wiser girl. Synonyms for *but* include *however, still,* and *nevertheless.*

Or emphasizes the alternative nature of the entities it joins, while *nor* emphasizes their (common) unsuitability. *Or* and *nor* are often found with their respective mates *either* and *neither,* where they are known as **correlative conjunctions**, the most common of which are:

either . . . or	not only . . . but also
neither . . . nor	whereas . . . therefore
both . . . and	whether . . . or

Either . . . or introduces two alternatives, either of which will do and only one of which is expected. They comprise the exclusive *or* of logic, that is, *either* but not *both.*

Neither . . . nor introduces excluded alternatives:

Neither snow, nor rain, nor heat, nor gloom of night stay these couriers from the swift completion of their appointed round.

Subordinating conjunctions make the clauses they introduce subordinate to, or dependent upon, the main clause of the sentence. Common **subordinating conjunctions** (and phrases) are:

after	because	since	when
although	before	so that	whenever
as	if	then	where
as if	inasmuch as	though	wherever
as long as	in order that	unless	whether
as though	provided that	until	while

Example: There is no point in discussing the matter, *since (because, as long as)* your mind is already made up.

Your mind is already made up is a perfectly good simple sentence, but slap a *since* in front of it and it cries out for a main clause either to precede or follow it. Clauses are not main, or subordinate, or supportive, or adversative in themselves—it is the conjunctions that introduce them that define their role.

> **Moral:** Give as much attention to these little words as to any other in your sentences.

One of the most common misusages is the use of *and* in place of *to* following the verb *try*. We should not try *and* do something, we should try *to* do it. This is an insidious little error. I do not include it in The Top Nine, but it bears watching.

Word Order

In the absence of inflection, word order provides an essential clue as to who did what to whom and why. As we have seen, except for pronouns (which we mutilate), we enjoy an almost complete dearth of inflection in English. The price we pay is that English word order is extremely important. In German, which is highly inflected, word order is relatively unimportant. Germans can, and often do, put their verbs at the very end of their sentences, as if to be sure the vehicle is totally assembled before adding the fuel.

Being used to it from birth, we find our word order "natural." In reality it is not natural at all, but it is necessary to avoid confusion and ambiguity. The immigrant German farmer thinks nothing of telling his helper: *Throw the cow over the fence some hay.* What has gone wrong here to

make us laugh? He has put the indirect object (the cow) immediately after the verb, as many textbooks tell us to do. Had he then followed this with the direct object (some hay) he would have said: *Throw the cow some hay.* A native could hardly do better. Instead, he chose to follow *cow* with the prepositional phrase *over the fence.* According to our rules, that makes *cow* the subject of that prepositional phrase and the game was lost. Forget about the hay!

We English experts, not having read the textbooks, would write: *Throw some hay over the fence,* and, to emphasize that the cow was the indirect object, we would add the prepositional phrase *to the cow.*

In the above example it was not a grammatical rule that forbade following the cow with a prepositional phrase. We could easily say: *Throw the cow by the tree some hay,* and no one would laugh. The real problem is that the sequence of words *throw-the-cow-over-the-fence* has in itself a literal and ludicrous interpretation, whereas *throw the cow by the tree* does not. As listeners we are constantly interpreting what we hear and waiting for the rest of the sentence to eliminate all but the intended meaning. The words *throw the cow* could have been followed by *with your lasso.* But *throw the cow over the fence* is such a graphic and arresting thought that it compels the listener to stop listening.

Out of this a simple rule emerges: Be sure that your words and their order do not lead the reader or listener to expect a meaning different from the one intended (in expository writing, at least; doing this misleading skillfully is the secret of many comedians). Your listener is trying, with your help, to get out of a maze. Don't lead her (or him) into blind alleys!

It is because we understand the meaning of words that we can disambiguate what we hear or read on the fly.

PITY THE POOR COMPUTER, WHICH WOULD FIND IT PERFECTLY ACCEPTABLE AND UN-FUNNY TO THROW THE COW OVER THE FENCE.

The reduction of the word order problem to a set of rules (as we attempted for pronunciation) is beyond our capabilities and perhaps beyond anyone's. In any case, this book would grow beyond your budget even if we succeeded. We must content ourselves with a few general principles and some advice. The primary requirement of expository writing or speech is that it be clear and unambiguous. It should also be as brief as possible and still meet this primary goal. This means that:

1. Modifiers should be close to the words they modify.

2. The antecedent for each pronoun (the thing it stands for) must be clear and unambiguous.

3. Conjunctions and clause order should be chosen to keep the main thought obvious and ancillary thoughts subordinate.

4. The sentences must develop a concept in an orderly way.

5. Remember that the reader does not know what is in your head, only what you have written.

Of all the admonitions above, the last is the most easily forgotten. Make a practice of trying to find another meaning to what you've written. If you can, others will, and often to your embarrassment.

The Power of Negative Unthinking (and Positive Thinking)

In English, negation follows the logic of algebraic multiplication. Now what the devil do I mean by that? Just that a negative associated with any quantity produces the opposite of that quantity. Further, *two* negatives associated with any quantity produce the *opposite of the opposite*, which leaves you where you started.

Most of us were taught quite early to avoid double negatives and gave up saying *don't never* as being the same as *never don't = always do*. Nevertheless, a surprising number of **double negatives** remain in our speech. How many of us commonly say, or catch ourselves about to say, incorrectly:

	Use Instead
can't hardly	can hardly
can't barely	can barely
can't help but (feel)	can't help (feeling)
haven't but (a moment)	have but (a moment)
haven't only	have only

Finally, many who avoid these traps succumb to the double negative hidden in the simple word *irregardless*. Starting with *regard*, meaning to consider or take into account, we add the suffix *-less* to obtain *regardless*, which means without considering or taking into account a clear negation. Then we add the prefix *ir-* meaning *not*—clearly a second negation—to produce *not without taking* into consideration, meaning we *do* take into consideration, that is, we are *regardful*. *Irregardless* is a nonword, thought to be an unconscious blend of *irrespective* and *regardless*. Forget you ever heard it!

There is a tendency to assume that negation obeys the laws of addition: The more negatives one throws in, the more negative the result, as if each negative were a check written on an already overdrawn account. It would be nice to be able to claim that English is consistent in this matter, but it is not. Apparently *repetition of the same negative* is construed as conferring emphasis rather than repeated reversals. Consider:

> **Never, NEVER, do that again!**
> **That's a no-no.**
> **No! No! A thousand times no!**

Moral: If you must use a double negative, stick to the same word.

Say What You Mean!

Phrases often pop into mind that sound fine but don't say exactly what you intend. Take the idiomatic: *I'm only thinking of the children.* If you are "only thinking" you are presumably doing nothing else. If you are *thinking only of the children*—which may be what you meant to say—not another subject is in your head. This seems like overkill. Perhaps what you really meant was: *My only concern is for the children.*

Your spouse is fretting about your imminent party and in particular whether you have enough coffee cups. You say: *Don't worry, everyone won't take coffee.* What you mean is: *Not everyone will have coffee.* There's a big difference. If the first be true, you needn't make any coffee.

The signs in the theater say: *No smoking allowed.* Literally, this means you are allowed *not* to smoke. It doesn't say *you must not.* The sign should read *smoking prohibited,* or *smoking not allowed.*

The attendant at the boarding gate announces: *Flight 157 is now ready for preboarding.* One would assume that *preboarding* was something to be done before boarding begins. But look, people are going through the gate! It must be that she really meant that Flight 157 is ready for *advance* boarding, that is, the boarding of children and disabled people *in advance* of those needing no help.

Like, As, As If

One of the most common errors in English is the use of *like* where *as* is called for. Although this problem grew worse following the hippies' incessant use of *like* as in *like cool, man*, the problem is not new. Fowler devotes several pages

to this issue and so, no doubt, will his successor in A.D. 2026. Part of the problem is that our ears have been conditioned since childhood to expect *like* whenever similarities are paraded:

> *like* a feather in the breeze
> we are going *like* sixty
> *like* a ton of bricks
> they taste *like* wine

The use of *like* becomes so natural that we use it when we shouldn't. In all the examples above, *like* (correctly) introduces a phrase or a noun. When a clause is to be introduced, formal English calls for the use of *as*:

As we agreed last Friday by telephone.
A is to B *as* C is to D.
Do as I say, not *as* I do.

In these examples, *we agreed last Friday* and *C is to D* are indeed clauses containing the verbs *agreed* and *is*. The third example shows that it is the verbs alone (I *say* and I *do*) that demand the *as*. A full clause is not needed. You mean to say it is that dumb little word that outlaws *like* and requires *as?* In a word, yes. Warriner[8] describes the matter as follows:

Like, as: *Like* is a preposition and introduces a prepositional phrase. *As* is usually a conjunction and introduces a subordinate clause.

He walks *like his father*.
(Prepositional phrase)

He walks *as his father walks*.
(Subordinate clause)

As a conjunction, *like* is commonly heard in informal speech, but it is unacceptable in formal English. If you find this argument appealing, use it and correct your correspondence accordingly. To me, *as* is a conjunction and *like* is a preposition because of their usage, not the other way around, so the argument seems circular.

What we really need is a simple test for whether *like* or *as* is needed. In a letter to William Safire,[9]

Priscilla Robertson of Lexington, Kentucky, complains that grammarians seem to offer *as* as the only alternative to *like*, and suggests that *the way* is often a less formal and equally grammatical alternative. Upon reading this, it struck me that here was the simple test I'd been looking for:

Simply substitute *the way* for *like* or *as*. If it fits, the proper choice is *as*:

        _____his father
        _____his father walks
        _____a cigarette should

Clearly, the last two require *as*. The trick here is that "the way" removes all aural prejudice for *like* and against *as*. As a synonym for *as*, it points out the need for the verb if *as* is to be used and, conversely, the need for *as* when the verb is there. In some cases, the appropriate replacement for *like* is *such as*. To quote Flanders and Swann on the subject of Portuguese Men-O-War:

I do not care to share the seas with jellyfishes such as these, particularly Portuguese.

Friendly Portuese Man-o-War in Monterey Bay

Do not use *like* to introduce subjunctive clauses; use *as if* (or *though*):

The children acted *as if* they were dead tired.

Careless Writing

Careless writing, like a neglected garden, tends to be cluttered, not with weeds but with useless words, tautologies (redundancies), and hackneyed phrases. Clear, vigorous prose strips the thought clean of such encumbrances, the better to reveal the salient facts. Not all dead wood is old; some of it is recent and some enjoy a remarkable popularity before heading into oblivion. Here are a few examples and suggested alternatives:

at this point in time | After a few years of haunting boardrooms and ad agencies, this tailor-made tautology landed on nationwide TV during the Watergate hearings and has spread like wildfire ever since. We assume this is because it offers a momentary pause while the speaker tries to figure out a meaningless answer to the last question. A "point in time" is a moment, so next time you could say *at this moment*. But English allows *at this time, at present*, or even better, *now*. That's only three letters.

decision as to whether | Let *whether* do its job. Or, if you use *decision*, neither *as to* nor *whether* is needed. In fact, just like *due to*, *as to* is a warning flag to get your pruning shears in hand.

due to the fact that | It is hard to find anything good to say about this venerable offender. When

you find five words that can be replaced by the single word *because* or *since*, you'd better remove them or the editor will. Most cases of *the fact that* can and should be replaced by shorter, better phrases.

Don't Say	Try
call attention to the fact that	remind
in spite of the fact that	although
the fact that he was bald	his baldness
I was unaware of the fact that	I didn't know that
the fact that she went	her going

Just inventing your way out of this bad habit can be fun.

however, thus | Many writers, especially scientists and engineers, feel obliged to lead the reader by the nose, as if the material were a mathematical proof. If the text is clear and straightforward, these guide words are unnecessary and make the prose sound pedantic. Try eliminating most of them.

needless to say | If true, don't say it. If not true, don't use the phrase.

Many instances of dead wood involve using a phrase in place of the single word you want. Often these are verb phrases introducing the noun form of the verb you want (or its opposite).

Original "Dead Wood"	Pruned Form
a period of a month	a month
conducted a poll	polled
held a meeting	met
in the near future	soon
not in favor of	opposed
put in an appearance	appeared
reached an agreement	agreed
take into consideration	consider

Unless you are getting paid by the word, the advantage of the pruned form is obvious.

PRUNING THE DEAD WOOD

Tautologies

A **tautology** is a phrase that says the same thing twice, in different ways.

Example: true fact
Facts are becoming more questionable, it seems, with each passing year. I was taught that the noun *fact* was reserved for those things that are true. If there was any doubt as to the veracity of a statement, we were not to use *fact*, but rather *allegation, belief, comment, myth, rumor, story, tale,* or *testimony.* Anything, in fact, that would not bias the reader.

Tautologies hang from our sentences like Spanish moss from mighty oaks. Here are some that most of us have been guilty of using.

Tautologies	Advice
add to a total of	Simply use *total*.
advanced planning	See preplanning.
advance reservations	No better than *reservations*.
any *and* all	Either will do.
assemble . . . *together*	No one assembles apart.
by *means of*	Means nothing more than *by*.
both . . . *also*	If you use *both*, don't follow it with *also* or *as well as*. For the second item, *and* will do.
check *into*	Only for hotel rooms.
consensus *of opinion*	A consensus *is* an agreement of opinions.
continue *to remain* cooperate *together* *customary* practice depreciate *in value*	As obvious as they are insidious.
different kinds	Kinds are already different.
each *and* every	An all-time favorite. If something is true of *each*, it is true of *every*, and vice versa.
end result	You can't get the *result* at half-time.
equally *as good as*	Equally implies as good as.
future prospects	What are your past prospects?
in order to	Just use *to*.
interpersonal relations	Typical personnel department talk.
joined *together*	Hard to do separately.
joint partnership	The best and only kind.
mental telepathy	As opposed to what other kind?

Tautologies	Advice
often accustomed to	Redundant, plain and simple.
often in the habit of	Do habits occur rarely?
past history	As opposed to Heinlein's stories?
preplanning	Planning should never be after the fact.
reason is *because*	Just tell us why.
repeat *again*	Okay if this is another repetition.
revert *back*	Try reverting ahead!
small *in size*	Size can be assumed.
strangled *to death*	Not just mildly?
up above	Somehow more obvious than down under.
up until	Well ingrained.
way, shape, or form	*Way* will do. The rest is habit.
ways *and* means	Classmate of *each and every*.
from whence	*Whence* means *from where*.

There are also a couple of **interlingual tautologies** one frequently hears:

and etc.	Since the *et* of *etc.* means *and* in Latin, this is pretty close to stammering.
please RSVP	The SVP stands for the French *s'il vous plait* (if you please). You might write *please R,* but I doubt if anyone would *respondez*.

These are perhaps more pardonable than all-English tautologies because of the user's unfamiliarity with the foreign phrase, but they still make our classic and French cognoscenti squirm.

Unnecessary Words

Closely related to tautologies are unnecessary words, such as in the use of superfluous prepositions.

Prepositions have a way of attaching themselves like barnacles to words that do very well on their own. In the following examples, the words in italics in the left-hand column are superfluous and can be eliminated to advantage.

continue *on*	*Continue* with your work.
converted *over*	*Converted* to metric units.
else but	No one *but* you could do it.
help *from*	They couldn't *help* applauding.
inside *of*	*Inside* the room . . .
like *for*	I would *like* you to . . .
near *to*	It's hanging *near* the door.
not *a* one	*Not one* or *no one*.
off *of*	He fell *off* the roof.
outside *of*	*Outside* the house.
over *with*	Be glad that's *over*.
pretend *like*	Don't *pretend* you don't know.

And finally, the winner: *up*. Take almost any verb and follow it with *up*.

act *up*	double *up*	mess *up*	show *up*
burn *up*	drink *up*	mix *up*	sign *up*
buy *up*	eat *up*	open *up*	size *up*
catch *up*	end *up*	pay *up*	start *up*
check *up*	finish *up*	polish *up*	strike *up*
climb *up*	fix *up*	rest *up*	talk *up*
cook *up*	follow *up*	run *up*	tear *up*
count *up*	hold *up*	scratch *up*	turn *up*
crumple *up*	hurry *up*	settle *up*	wake *up*
divide *up*	lift *up*	shape *up*	write *up*

Not all of these *up*'s are useless. Many add a shade of meaning to the verb. For example, *catch up* has a more specific meaning than *catch*, namely to no longer be behind. Likewise, *hold up* has many meanings that *hold* alone does not. Nevertheless, it pays to examine these little verb-followers to see if they add clarity or are merely colloquial.

Without question, phrases like *in a very real sense . . ., it should be pointed out that . . ., it is interesting to note that . . .* serve only to encourage the writer that what he is writing makes sense, is worthwhile, or is interesting. They do nothing for the reader. Say only what makes sense, point out what you must, and be interesting about it. No need to warn us in advance.

Vogue Words and Phrases

Words come and go. Some burst on the scene overnight, spend their short lives overused, and disappear suddenly. Fowler calls these *vogue words* and warns against their use. If you are writing

something ephemeral, like the monthly gossip club news, use these words freely if they seem appropriate, but if you expect your writing to endure, eschew them. Writing with **vogue words** is like using disappearing ink. Some examples are:

attrit	Verb made by curtailing the noun *attrition*.
bottom line	How to render an MBA speechless: forbid "bottom line."
definitize	How about *specify*?
finalize	We used to say *complete*.
impact	How does this strike you?
into	To be interested in.
incentivize	Used to be *motivate*. Will soon be again.
ongoing	Teachers' pet word for *never-ending*.
prioritize	Fancy word for *rank*.

Sometimes the popularity of a vogue word or phrase reaches astonishing proportions. An example, only a few years old, is the continual interjection of *y'know* into otherwise normal speech. Many times I have been tempted to shout (necessary to stanch the hemorrhage of words), "If *I know*, why are you telling me?" My psychiatrist friends assured me that this habit was simply a subconscious attempt of the young person not to appear didactic. Well, I knew there was *some* reason.

Another problem is the limitation of the number of adjectives at the speaker's command to only two. At one time, these were *gross* and *fantastic*. Earlier, *boss* had a brief ascendancy.

A recent plague is the use of the verb *go* in place of *said*. "Then I *go* blah blah blah. Then he *goes*, No kidding! Then I *go*, etc., etc." Pretty soon I want to go myself.

These epidemics usually originate among our young people, especially those still in schools or colleges. There's nothing new about the phenomenon and, in my opinion, nothing to worry about except as it implies a lack of ability to use English. I seem to recall that before World War II, we had words and phrases like *hip*, then *hep*, and *zoot* as in *zoot suit*. Then there was an epidemic of *copasetic*. But by then I was too old to enjoy secret societies anymore.

No, it is not the onslaught of slang that concerns me most. Useless words will die and only the useful survive to become tomorrow's English. That is the way languages renew themselves. I certainly prefer a *laissez-faire* attitude to the French Academy's practice of censoring new additions to French.

The spoken word is a fleeting sound that dies away even as it is uttered. To preserve the edicts of kings, to memorialize tribal victories, to substantiate anything from rules of conduct to a new tax rate, something more permanent is needed. Today we can record and reproduce electronically the actual sounds of speech, but even with these riches, we still feel the need of a portable, permanent record to peruse at our leisure.

The earliest writings were pictures of the memorable events themselves, such as those found in the cave paintings at Lascaux, France.

Then, as early as the third millennium B.C., we find the ancient Egyptian hieroglyphics and the early Persian and Sumerian cuneiform pictographs. With time, and because the precise meaning of pictures is not obvious, the drawings became stylized. The ideographs of classic Chinese are a form of picture writing that survives to this day.

The shortcomings of picture writing are its vagueness and the enormous range of symbols needed to express even the smallest range of human thought. Eventually, the scribes simplified the pictures and began to use them to signify not the thought but the initial sound, say, of the object pictured. Our letter *G* comes from the Greek *gamma*, whose upper-case symbol is Γ. This symbol is the picture used almost two thousand years ago in early Hebrew for *gimel*, or as we say: *camel*.

This conversion from using complex pictures (to represent one of countless *thoughts*) and later simple pictures (to represent the few *sounds* of a language) to alphabetic writing was the real break-through. Authors, publishers, and librarians, please bow your heads.

English uses about forty elementary sounds, or phonemes (more if you are really fussy), so an alphabet of forty characters would do us nicely. We could then have a simple one-to-one correspondence between sound and symbol, and learning to read would be child's play. Literally. But, with only twenty-six letters at our disposal, some must do double duty, modifying the sounds of their neighbors in ways that are neither simple nor regular. As a result, most children need, and often do not get, proper help in learning to read. The problem is that most teachers in this epoch believe that English pronunciation is so irregular that there is no point in trying to identify or teach rules. We think this is an overstatement, that there is more regularity than they think, and that even a little helps a lot since, with exceptions, word groups can be taught as families. Also, it is not in reading the common short words that the child is apt to need help. Rather, it is in tackling the rarer, longer words, which are more regular in pronunciation. In any case, we have included a few rules, for your sake and perhaps for your child's sake.

Half of learning to read well is developing an instantaneous association of the letters and letter groups with the sounds. Alphabetic writing is simply a code for describing the sounds of vocal speech. So we have little interest in the *names* of the letters, only the sounds they stand for. If we display *s*, don't think of *ess*, think of *s-s-s-s*. The sound's the thing. Also, the terms *short* and *long*, as applied to vowels, refer not to the duration of the sound but to its tonal quality. The "short" *o*, as in *hot*, and the "long" *o*, as in *bone*, differ in tone or timbre—that is, in the way their energy is distributed in their spectra—not necessarily in their duration.

The classical division of the sounds of speech is into *vowels* and *consonants*. As your teacher once said, "The vowels are *a, e, i, o, u,* and sometimes *y.*" But she probably told you little or nothing about why a particular sound was a vowel. In *voiced* speech, we modulate the spectrum of a complex buzz-tone generated by our vocal cords. In *unvoiced* sounds, and in all of whispered speech, the vocal cords are slack, and only the rushing sound of the escaping air is modulated (modified) by the changing resonances of our vocal tract. To all this we add a plethora of puffs, hisses, and wheezes produced by constricting the air flow at various points along its way.

All these latter sounds are transient consonants, but *m, n,* and *r*—come on, sounds only! *m-m-m-m, n-n-n-n,* and *r-r-r-r*—are sustainable voiced sounds, the latter made with the lips open. With all this diversity, what unique quality defines a vowel? We think the answer is:

RULE #1
In English, each syllable contains one vowel or diphthong sound, and conversely, each vowel sound defines a syllable.

Note that this rule applies to the *sounds*, not to the vowel letters. Because of our history or because we have too few graphemes (symbols), we may use more than one letter per vowel sound. But there will be only one vowel sound per syllable. As a rule, long words tend to fall apart into these syllables, and hyphens bother us least if they occur at the natural breaks between syllables. Learning to read and spell words may be speeded and facilitated by prior practice in learning to read and spell syllables with ease, which in fact is what some phonics-based methods do. Consonants, as the name implies, are *sounded with* the vowel sound to complete the syllable.

Vowel sounds and syllables differ greatly from language to language, but all tongues require them. Even Polish, which looks like interminable strings of consonants, has vowel sounds hidden among them. Japanese make the most regular use of vowels of any major language. Except for vowels like long *o* and long *i* (pronounced *ee*), which can stand alone, all syllables are two letters long, beginning with a consonant and ending with a vowel. Since only forty-seven or forty-eight such combinations are used, it is more efficient to write Japanese syllable by syllable rather than letter by letter. That is precisely what the *Iroha* (the Japanese syllabary) does. The name comes from the first three syllables listed, *ee, roh, hah*—just as our alphabet takes its name from the first two Greek letters: *alpha* and *beta*.

Table I is an attempt to classify the vowel sounds of English. We have chosen to use as few diacritical marks as we could, preferring instead to illustrate the sound by words containing no pronunciation ambiguity. We have also tried, in these examples, to include all the ways the sound is written. For example, the short sound of *e* is given by the letter itself in *bed*, by *ai* in *said*, and by *ea* in *head*. Notice that the letters active in producing the vowel sound are printed in **boldface**.

TABLE I
English Vowel Sounds

Symbol	Examples	
	Short Vowel Sounds	
a	c**a**t, d**a**d, m**a**n	
e	b**e**d, p**e**t, s**ai**d, h**ea**d	
i	**i**f, **i**t, s**i**t, w**i**th, m**y**th	
o	c**o**t, h**o**p, c**a**lm, f**a**ther, c**a**r	
o	l**o**g, m**o**th, t**a**lk, s**a**w, f**au**n, g**o**ne, **ou**ght	
oo	b**oo**k, l**oo**k, g**oo**d, w**oo**l	
u	d**u**d, d**o**ne, l**o**ve, r**ou**gh, d**ou**ble, ban**a**na	
	Long Vowel Sounds	
e	f**ee**t, s**ea**t, l**ea**d, br**ie**f, s**ei**ze, k**e**y, h**e**re	
o	g**o**, h**o**me, r**oa**d, h**oe**d, f**o**lk, s**ou**l, sl**o**w, d**oo**r, d**ou**gh	
oo	m**oo**n, t**oo**t, m**o**ve, sl**ou**gh, s**ou**p, d**o**, bl**ue**, s**ui**t	
	Diphthongs	Composition
a	**a**te, br**ea**k, r**ai**n, r**ei**n, **ei**ght, h**e**y, p**a**y	a = eh-ee
i	k**i**te, s**igh**, l**ie**, sk**y**, **eye**	oe = ah-ee
ow	h**ow**, n**ow**, c**ow**, **ou**t, b**ough**	o-oo = ah-ooh
oi	**oi**l, b**oy**, t**oy**	ô-ee = aw-ee
u	c**u**te, m**u**le, y**ou**, **ewe**, h**ue**	e-oo = ee-ooh

Notice that most of the vowel sounds can be written in several ways. Conversely, many of these written equivalents can represent more than one vowel sound. The classic example is the all-purpose combination *ough*, which is *oh* in *dough*, *off* in *cough*, *oo* in *slough*, *aw* in *ought*, *ow* in *bough*, and *uff* in *rough*. To a computer scientist, it seems absurd to use more than one code for the same object or have such ambiguity in the objects represented by the same code. This is the basis for the charges of irregularity and lawlessness of which our language is accused.

ALMOST EVERY WORD
IS AN OUTLAW!

These are the irrationalities that prove English to be the result of historical accident and compromise—to be E.B. White's cow path, in short—rather than a logical work of art.

YOU MUST REMEMBER THAT ENGLISH IS THE RESULT OF HISTORICAL ACCIDENT AND COMPROMISE... NOT A LOGICAL WORK OF ART.

TABLE I IS AN ATTEMPT TO CLASSIFY THE VOWEL SOUNDS OF ENGLISH.

We could, in principle, tidy up our spelling into a regular phonetic system, as the Japanese do. The cost would be to send us all back to the first grade. Also, we would lose the advantage that homophones provide—words that sound alike but whose different spellings clarify their meaning. In addition, we would lose a lot of history. For each of you who may be annoyed that *-tion* is pronounced *shun* in many words, I can find others delighted to discover that all such words came into English from the French during the Norman invasion. Originally they were pronounced as they are still spelled: *a-c-t-i-o-n* was pronounced *ak-tee-ong*. Time has corrupted our pronunciation, but we have retained the spelling.

THE NORMANDY INVASION OF ENGLAND IN 1066 LED EVENTUALLY TO THE MERGING OF NORMAN FRENCH WITH ANGLO-SAXON GERMANIC TO BECOME ENGLISH. ACTION, ORIGINALLY PRONOUNCED "AK-TEE-ONG," BECAME "AK-SHUN".

"WILLIAM THE CONQUEROR" PROBABLY PRONOUNCED IT "ACK-TEE-ONG."

Table I differs from many phonetic classifications, mainly in the cause of simplicity. We show the sound of *a* as in *father* as a short *o*. This is somewhat of a fielder's choice. Do you hear any difference between *father* and *bother*? Many would call the long sound of *oo*, as in *boot*, the long *u* sound, as in *rude*. But more often the long *u* sound is a diphthong *ee-oo*, as in *cute* or *mute*, so it seems simpler to define them this way. If you like, Table I is the way my ear hears U.S. Grade-A speech.

A diphthong is a two-faced vowel; it begins as one sound and ends as another. We know it by neither of these terminal sounds, but by the transient sound in the middle. Try saying long *i* slowly. You begin by saying *ah* and end by saying *ee*. In between, the diphthong slips out. You can prolong the *ah* and the *ee* all you wish, but what we call the *i* sound appears only as the *ah* is fading and the *ee* appearing. As Table I shows, many so-called long vowels are really diphthongs. By the way, it's pronounced *diff-thong*, not *dip-thong*, just as it's *diff-theria*, not *dip-theria*. *Diff*, not *dip*.

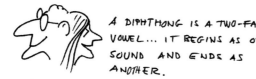

A DIPHTHONG IS A TWO-FACED VOWEL... IT BEGINS AS ONE SOUND AND ENDS AS ANOTHER.

Table II classifies the consonants according to the nature of their sounds and whether they are *voiced* or *unvoiced*. The *plosives* are accomplished by the release of a tiny puff of air. You can feel it if you place your hand in front of your mouth as you pronounce them. They are all transient sounds.

TABLE II
English Consonant Sounds

Unvoiced		Category	Voiced	
		Transient	l	level
ch	chug, catch	Plosives	j	jug, badge
p	pay, papa		b	bay, baba
t	toe		d	doe
k	cat, kink, cirque		g	gone
x	= ks	Sibilant	x	excite
s	sip, city		z	zip
sh	ash		zh	azure
f	file, laugh, photo	Fricatives	v	vial
th	think, bath		th	the, father
h	ham, hover	Breathy	y	yes
w	wand, water, wind			
wh	where, while			
		Open	r	girl
		Closed	m	mama
			n	nono

The *sibilants* are the hissing sounds of our speech. They are shriller and tend to be more tonal than the *fricatives*, which sound like smooth surfaces rubbing. The sounds we have called *breathy*—some would say *windy*—are made with the vocal tract open and with a soft but audible rushing sound. When *y* is called a consonant, as in *yes*, the sound can also be considered a vowel sound of short duration. Thus, *yes = ee-ss*, and *wand = oo-ahnd*. The pair *wh* adds more air flow and perhaps should be written *hw*. Next, we list the vowel-like consonant *r*, and take its sound to be not the same as the letter, *ah-er*, but the sustainable whirring sound that persists after the introductory *ah* has faded away. Finally, we list the consonants *m* and *n*, which call for a closed vocal tract, at the lips for *m*, and by the tongue for *n*.

If **Rule #1** is a good rule, it should hold for the two words in English that are one letter long. Indeed, they are both vowels: the indefinite article *a* and the first person singular pronoun, *I*. By convention the latter is always capitalized and takes the long sound (*ah-ee*). The former, *a*, is capitalized if it begins a sentence. Its pronunciation varies from the long *a* sound to the short *u* sound, as in *about*. This is called the *schwa* sound and has the symbol ∂ in the international phonetic alphabet. All vowels can be said to tend toward a *schwa* as the stress laid on them decreases.

The number is slightly arbitrary, but there are nearly sixty two-letter words, about equally divided between those with the vowel first and the vowel last.

With **beginning vowels** we have:

ad(d)	ed	id	odd	ugh
ah	egg	if	of(f)	uh
am	el	in	[oh]	um
an	em	is	on	up
as	en	it	or	us
at	er		os	ux
axe			ow	

Those with **final vowels** are:

da	be	by	go	[do]
ha	he	die	ho	[to]
la	me	dye	lo	
ma	re	fi	no	
pa	she	hi	so	
ta	the	my		
	ye	shy		
		xi		

We have listed a few three-letter words in which the added letter merely doubles the consonant or is part of a consonant digraph, like *sh* or *th*. Parentheses in these cases indicate that there is a two-letter word without the added consonant. We now notice a surprising regularity:

RULE #2
If a two-letter word begins with a vowel or ends in *a*, the vowel is short; if it ends in a vowel other than *a*, the vowel is long.

Notice that the words ending in *a* all take the short *o* sound, as in *hot*, which is a common or "regular" sound for *a*. The long *o* in *oh* and the words *do* and *to* in the last column that take the long sound of *oo* are the only real exceptions to the rule and are put in brackets.

A consonant blend is any pair of consonants written together and pronounced without an intervening vowel—pairs like *bl, br, cr,* and *cl.* If we allow consonant blends and digraphs before or after the vowel, we can add forty more words with no exceptional cases. So here we are with one hundred words, only three of which we have to call exceptions or outlaws.

Next we consider three-letter words with a beginning and ending consonant and a central vowel—words like *bat, cat,* and *did.* There are about 276 of these, so we don't list them all. If we allow blended consonants at the beginning—words like *drab* and *clad*—we get 151 more for a total of 427. All the vowels have their short sounds and, by our standards, all are regular. (We're now at 527 words. When does the trouble start?)

To get the long vowel sounds in these words, and to add many words with no short vowel counterpart, we do one of two things: In the case of *e* we double the letter. Thus *wed* becomes *weed, pep* becomes *peep,* and so on.

For all other vowels, we add the *e,* not just after the vowel but at the end of the word. Thus *cap* becomes *cape, hop* becomes *hope.*

In this way, we can add about four hundred more words to our list, for a grand total of over a thousand words. Are there no exceptions? Yes, a few. In *here, mere, sere,* and *sphere,* the long *e* is obtained not by doubling the *e,* but by adding one at the end. Adding the final *e* after the vowel *a* gives us many words like *wave, save,* and *gave.* But *a* refuses to become long in *have.* Similarly with *i,* the final *e* makes *kite* out of *kit,* but it doesn't make the *i* long in *live* and *give*—and in their derivatives like *liver* and *giver.* In the case of *o,* the exceptions are so numerous that we avoid them by making a better rule. The final *e* makes the *o* long in many words like *bone* and *home.* In many others, like *come, done,* and *love,* it produces the short *u* sound. Well, if we can't lick 'em, let's join 'em and write the rule this way:

RULE #3
In a consonant-vowel-consonant syllable, the vowel is short. To make the vowel long in the case of *e,* it is doubled; for *a, i,* or *u,* a final *e* is added; and for *o,* the final *e* either makes the vowel long or gives it the sound of short *u.*

This is not mere game playing. The rule has few exceptions (*have, live, give, gone*), and the uncertainty in the case of *o* is at most only one bit, for the pupil is faced with only a binary choice. This is much better than having to guess with no help at all.

In doing its task of modifying the earlier vowel sound, the final *e* remains silent. Thus we end up with words like *babe* and *lade*. But suppose we want a final long *e* sound, what do we do then? Why, that's one of the great uses of *y*. Simply substitute it for the *e*, and you get *baby* and *lady*. Notice that here the sound of *y* is a long *e*, while in monosyllables like *sky* it takes the long *i* sound. Well, a character has to dress for the occasion. The long *e* sound of a final *y* is the rule for long words, such as all adverbs ending in *-ly*.

As we might expect, the influence on the previous vowel of an *e* separated by a single consonant is not limited to our short single syllables. There are obvious cases like *makeshift* or *Capetown,* in which we recognize our old short word at the beginning of the longer one. But the rule holds generally. Furthermore, the second vowel need not be an *e*. Take the case of *radio.* Unless you are Al Smith, the *a* is long.

Now that we see what makes vowels long in long words, how can we prevent it? Why, very simply:

RULE #4
To restore the short sound of a vowel in spite of an encroaching following vowel, double the consonant between them.

Thus, *diner* becomes *dinner, holy* becomes *holly,* and *scraper* becomes *scrapper.*

It is interesting that the two consonants of a digraph do not afford the "insulation" from the final *e* needed to keep the vowel short. Thus, we have words like *lathe* and *bathe.* We also have *table, cradle, bridle,* and many other words ending in *-le* (pronounced *ul*). To recover the short initial vowel sound, we still must double the consonants, as in *dabble, addle,* and *fiddle.*

As an experienced reader, you will recognize that just as there is a large family of words ending in *-ble, -dle, -fle, -gle, -nkle, -ple, -sle, -tle,* and even *-zle,* so there are families of words for each example given for each vowel sound in Table I. If we call "regular" only the examples at the beginning of each line (*cat, bed, if, hat,* etc.), then all the families of words later in the lines are irregular, and English is truly a language full of exceptions. Indeed, we have made it so, in a sense. We have made the laws so restrictive that almost every word's an outlaw!

But what is wrong with making our laws much broader? What is wrong with accepting as regular citizens all the vowel spellings given in Table I? The price of having these spellings has already been paid in the way of ambiguity and coding inefficiency. We do not improve matters by ignoring them. Of course, we will increase the number of rules we must teach, but we must teach the facts even if we don't call them rules. The great value of extending our rule set is that many words are learned at once as a now legitimate family. And, of course, we can go too far. There's no point in calling the legislature into session for one or two exceptions. So call *have, live,* and *give* outlaws, and let's get on with the story!

Vowels are not the only sounds with multiple representations. Examination of Table II shows the plosive *ch* is sometimes *-tch* as in *catch,* while its voiced equivalent is given both ways in *judge.* The *k* sound can be represented by *c, k, ck,* or *que,* while the fricative *f* is sometimes written as *gh* or *ph.* Whether *s* and *th* are voiced or not seems to depend on their position in the word. Initial *s*'s are generally unvoiced, and final single *s*'s are often voiced, as in the suffixes *-ise* and *-ism.*

Some consonants have a strong effect on the vowels that precede them. Examples are *l* and *w,* which give the associated *a* the *aw* sound, as in *walk, war,* and *talk.* Many phonicians hear a strong influence from *r.* They distinguish between the long *a* sound followed by *r* and the vowel sound in *air.*

The letter *g* has a profound effect on the preceding *n,* producing the "nasal *n*" sound in which the tongue held against the roof of the mouth closes off all mouth air flow. Thus we obtain the "ringing" sound of *sang, sing, song,* and *seeing.* The word *length* has an *ng* in it, but many people, especially from New York or New Jersey, omit the *g* and say *lenth.* (They also have trouble blending *l* and *n,* and speak of a *lenth* of *fill-um.*) So unless

you're trying to play a character from Flatbush or Hoboken, be sure to observe the *g* clue for a nasal *n.* Make *length ring.*

While we're on the subject of dimensions, there's another common error in pronunciation we should mention. It's leng*th,* wid*th,* bread*th,* dep*th,* but it's not heigh*th.* There's no such word. The word is heigh*t.* No *th* ending in sight! By the way, this word is about the only exception to *eigh* saying long *a.* If I were to alter the word, I'd remove the *e,* leaving *hight.*

RULE #5
The letter *c* takes the *s* sound when followed by *e, i,* or *y.* At all other times it says *k.*

Now there's a rule you should know. Not only is it useful, it is also obeyed almost without exception. Let's look at a few words. In *cycle,* the first *c* is before *y* so it says *s.* The second is before *l* and says *k.* Check! In *account,* neither *c* precedes an *e, i,* or *y,* so they both say *k.* Double check! In *accept,* the first *c* precedes a *c,* while the second precedes an *e.* So the pronunciation is *ak-sept.* Right? So also are the words *succeed* (*suck-seed*), *succinct* (*suck-singt*), and *accelerate* (*ack-sell-er-ate*). (Notice in *succinct* the final *-ct* makes the preceding *n* nasal, as a *g* or *k* would.)

When adding suffixes to words, the general rule is that the suffix should not alter the sound of the root word. In particular, the vowel should remain long or short. Thus, in adding *-ing* to *run* we must double the *n* and write *running.* Conversely, if the root ends in *e,* making the vowel long, we can usually drop the *e* when the suffix begins with a vowel. Thus *like* becomes *likable*. Most exceptions occur because of **Rule #5**. For example, we cannot change *dance* into *dancable*. We must write *danceable*, for we do not want the reader saying *dankable*, as **Rule #5** would demand. For words ending in *c*, like *traffic* or *garlic*, we need to keep the *k* sound, and this is done by adding *k* to make *trafficking* or *garlicked*. An exception seems to be the single syllable *arc*, for which *arced, arcing*, etc., seem to be preferred. Other words, like *critic-criticize* and *toxic-toxicity*, do not add a *k*, preferring rather to let the *c* take the *s* sound, so in a sense they are not exceptions.

The accent or stress given different syllables of a word is an important aspect of pronunciation and is indicated in dictionaries along with other diacritical marks defining the pronunciation. Incorrect accenting is often the mark of one who has learned English by reading rather than listening. Some examples of commonly misaccented words are given at the end of this section.

The common tendency in English is to stress the earlier part of the word rather than the middle or end. Thus we say, *dis-TRIB-ute* rather than *dis-trib-UTE*. There also is a tendency to stress the root word rather than its prefixes or suffixes, except when the main thought line is determined by the prefix. Thus we have *in-ter-de-PEND-ent* with the accent on the next to last syllable to keep the prefixes *inter-* and *de-* intact. But we also have *AD-vo-ca-cy*, where the prefix tells that the action was for, not against.

Most of us realize that English words can often serve as different parts of speech. We are less aware that we often change the accent in the process. Thus the verb meaning *to stick out* is pronounced *proh-JECT* while the noun meaning *what we are working on* is pronounced *PRAH-ject*. So too we have *CON-tent* (the volume of a container) and *con-TENT* (to be at peace). This change in emphasis can be regarded as a primitive form of inflection that helps to distinguish the two meanings. It does not seem to be a source of confusion, so we will not pursue it, but it is of interest that our speech is perhaps a little more inflected than we may have thought.

Reluctantly, we must either abandon our brief analysis of spelling and pronunciation or else devote the book to the subject. Those who might like to dig deeper may try reading the section at the beginning of the dictionary, preferably an unabridged *Webster's*—noting that each updated version reveals the changes that have taken place in our language.

Miscellaneous Mispronunciations

Here are a number of words that are often mispronounced. The list is not complete, nor could it ever be—it's just those words that happen to have lodged in my memory. Perhaps listing them here will be cathartic.

arthritis | *Arthron* means joint in Greek, and *itis* is doctor talk for inflammation of. So *arthritis*, as any victim will tell you, is inflammation of the joints, not an ailment that Arthur has.

ask | Please do not invert the order of the *s* and *k*, producing *axe*. When you say, "I'll axe her," it gives a definite Lizzie Borden impression, and one we don't need. Sloppy California diction drops the *k* and turns the word into *ass*. The same holds for *bask, mask, task, tusk,* etc. Practice saying the *plural* of each of these with an *audible k* and an *audible s* both before and after the *k*. Listen: *mass - k - sss*.

asterisk | Not *ass-trick*, as appealing as that may sound to you. From the Greek *asteriskos*, diminutive of *aster*, a star.

> *Mary donned her shiny skates*
> *And went on the ice to frisk.*
> *Wasn't she a silly girl,*
> *Landing on her * ?*

athlete | This word seems determined to pick up an extra syllable in its middle. It's simply *ath-lete*, not *ath-a-lete*, and *ath-letics*, not *ath-a-letics*. See *realtor*.

au gratin | Perhaps it's not fair to include an undigested French morsel, but the phrase is so common, we should do better. It's not *aw-grattin*, it's *oh-grahTAAA*. Note to Francophiles: I know it should be a virtually unvoiced nasal *n*, as in *vin*, but how do I write it?

au jus | Again, not *aw* but *oh*: *oh-zhoo*. (Note: *zh = z* as in *azure*.)

a whole 'nother | Strictly speaking, this is not just mispronunciation; it's a grammatical inversion involving a nonexistent word. But I didn't know where else to put it. Make it *another whole*, please.

canned | Pronounce the final *-ed*. Most people don't and, as a result, my grocery store displays *can* goods.

contributory | Should be pronounced to rhyme with *tory*, not *Terry*. On the other hand, a little river that joins a big one is a *tributary*.

couldn't, wouldn't, shouldn't | Some people drop the *d* sound in these and similar words to obtain *coont, woont, shoont,* etc., with the *oo* as in *roof*. The apostrophe tells you the *o* of *-not* has been omitted. Pronounce the words as if you *could, would,* or *should* and add the *-unt* at the end. Takes a little longer, but avoids quizzical glances.

dilettante | Many people, assuming the word to be of French origin, make the last part rhyme with *aunt*. But it's of Italian origin and should rhyme with *auntie*.

etc. | Abbreviation for the Latin *et cetera*, meaning *"and others similar,"* equivalent to *and so forth.* There's not an *ex* anywhere to be seen, so don't call it *ex cetera.*

exit, example | There is a tendency today to voice the *k* in *eks,* which immediately turns it into *eggs.* Liberal dictionaries may show both pronunciations, but I prefer *ek-sit* to *egg-sit* and *eks-ample* to *egg-sample.* The low-cholesterol original seems cleaner, less messy.

extraterrestrial | Same problem as with *terrestrial* (see below), but more so.

February | The child's habit of dropping the first *r* in this word lingers into adulthood far too often. Come on, let's get it right: *Feb-brew-wary* (see *library*).

jewelry | It's *jewel-ree,* not *joo-ler-ee.*

liaison | There's no end of trouble with this little word—almost as much as with the sort of relation it implies. The usual mispronunciation is *LAY-is-on.* No one who knows any phonics (and that should now include you) would ever dream that *ia* could say long *a* (see Table I). *Ai* perhaps, as in *rain,* and indeed that's what the *-ai-* says in this word. Break it up this way: *li-ai-son* and say *lee-AY-zawn.* (To get an A+ give that last *n* the French nasal bit.)

library | It's *lie-brer-y* not *lie-berry,* as we both know you've been told (see *February*).

lingerie | Macy's and Gimbel's seem to have agreed on *lawn-jer-ay,* so we can be sure something's wrong. We'd be closer simply to Anglicize or Americanize the word and say *lynn-ger-ee.* But aside from the French *-in* as in *vin,* there's really nothing to it: *lanh-zher-ee.* The only problem with saying it correctly is in being understood.

mirror | Commonly mispronounced *mere.* I have a longtime friend (a writer of both fact and fiction) who pronounces the word to rhyme with John Muir. The word has two syllables and is pronounced *mere-roar* or *mere-er.* Either will do, but don't cut off the tail!

nuclear | Don't swallow, it's simply *new + clear.* Where Ike got *nuke-you-ler,* I'll never know, but we are not obliged to imitate him.

poinsettia | *Poyn-set-ee-ah,* or *poyn-SET-tcha,* but not *poyn-set-uh.*

process | There is very little trouble with this word in its singular form. The accent for the noun is on the first syllable. The short *o* sound is preferred in the U.S., but the long *o* is often heard, especially in Britain.

processes | The trouble is with the plural form, where a surprising number of technical people, enamored of the plural *axes* for *axis, analyses* for *analysis, crises* for *crisis,* and so on, conclude that the plural of *process* must be *pro-cess-eez.*

Never mind that *process* does not end in *-is* and is *not* Greek. Don't listen to these amateur etymologists. *Processes* rhymes with *recesses, abscesses,* and *confesses.*

Q.E.D. | *Quod erat demonstrandem,* Latin for "as was to be demonstrated." In olden days, no proof was complete without this assertion.

realtor | It's nice if you say *real-tawr* (rhyming with *more*) rather than *real-terr*, but don't add an *i* in the middle. It's not *real-i-tor*, it's *real-tor*, a simple consonant blend of *l* and *t* as in *halter.*

subsidiary | The word is *sub-SIDDY-airy*, not *sub-SIDDER-EE* or *sub-SIDDER-airy.*

succinct | Why this word isn't recognized as being like *accent* or *success*, I'll never know.

terrestrial The final *r* is often dropped, but shouldn't be.

(*n.* = noun; *v.* = verb; *adj.* = adjective)

accent | *n.* The peculiarities in pronunciation associated with region, race, or national origin. Also, *v.* To stress a particular syllable in a word.

active (voice) | *adj.* The construction and word order used to assert that the subject performs the action described by the verb. See **passive**.

adjective | *n.* A word that modifies a noun, as in a *white* horse.

adverb | *n.* A word that modifies a verb or an adjective, as in a *poorly* performed part.

agreement | *n.* Two word forms coinciding in person, number, tense, case, etc., as required by the grammar.

antecedent | *n.* The earlier named person, place, or thing that is later represented by a pronoun.

antonym | *n.* A word of opposite meaning: *glorious* is the antonym of *shameful*.

appositive | *n.* A noun or noun phrase referring to the same person or thing, as in a biography of the *poet, Burns.* Two appositives are said to stand in apposition and one is set off by commas.

article | *n.* A word such as *a, an,* or *the* that precedes a noun and indicates its generality (*a, an*) or specificity (*the*) with respect to the thought being expressed.

auxiliary | *n.* A word that helps another. The auxiliary of a verb often gives the time relationship, as in: If he misses the meeting, he *will have been* absent four times.

blend | *n.* or *v.* A pair of elementary sounds pronounced in direct succession without an intervening pause or sound. The letters *dr* in *drip* are a consonant blend.

case | *n.* The generic term for the relation of nouns and pronouns to the verbs and prepositions of a sentence. The cases in English are the nominative, objective, and possessive.

clause | *n.* A clause is a group of words, complete with a subject and predicate, that expresses a thought auxiliary to that of the sentence containing it.

collective nouns | *n.* Words that name a group of persons or things. The tendency is to consider these nouns as singular in the United States and plural in England.

colon | *n.* The punctuation mark used after a salutation, or to introduce a formal statement, list, or example.

comma | *n.* The most common punctuation mark, used to indicate a pause to the reader and to separate nonrestrictive clauses, words in a list, etc.

comparison of modifiers | *n.* The change in form (or the use of auxiliary words) to indicate the relative magnitude of the modification produced by an adjective or adverb, as in *happy* (positive form), *happier* (comparative form), *happiest* (superlative form).

compound | *n.* Composed of more than one item.

conjugate | *v.* To give, in a systematic order, the various forms of a word, especially the forms of the different tenses of a verb. The list, so ordered, is called the **conjugation** (*n.*) of the verb.

conjunction | *n.* A word that serves to connect two other words, phrases, or clauses while indicating the relation between them.

consonant | *n.* From the Latin *con* (*with*) and *sonare* meaning *to sound.* All letters of the alphabet that are sounded with the vowels to form words or syllables.

dangling | *adj.* Said of a word or phrase whose relation to the sentence is either ambiguous or absent. Example: *Carrying a heavy armload of books, his toe caught on the carpet. Carrying* is a **dangling participle.** Was *his toe* carrying the books? The addition of *while he was* at the beginning would end the tangle and the dangle.

decline | *v.* To give, in a systematic order, the various forms of a noun, pronoun, or adjective required by its case, gender, and number, that is, its *inflection.* The result is the **declension** of the word.

digraph | *n.* A pair of letters that together produce a single sound different from the sound of either letter alone. Examples: *th* as in *thick, sh* as in *ash.* (Note: In cryptography, a digraph is *any* two adjacent letters.)

diphthong | *n.* A vowel whose beginning and ending sounds differ and whose characteristic sound is the transition between the two. Example: Long *i* is the diphthong *ah-(i)-ee.*

double negative | *n.* Two terms of negation used so that (according to the rules of the language) their effects are canceled, leaving a positive statement. Example: *It doesn't mean nothing to me.* If it doesn't mean *nothing,* it must mean *something.*

ellipsis | *n.* The omission of letters in a word or of words in a sentence. The omission of letters is indicated by an apostrophe. Example: *can't = can(no)t.* The omission of words (usually a clause or two irrelevant to the discussion) is indicated by three dots. Example: *He said that . . . he was not going.* Omitted words: *. . . on his sister's advice . . .*

exclamation point | *n.* A punctuation mark used to indicate emphasis, especially when due to surprise or excitement. An instruction of dubious merit to the reader to wake up! A confession by the writer that the situation merits more attention than his words suggest. Use sparingly. Make your words exclaim.

expletive | *n.* A word or phrase unnecessary to the grammar or thought of the sentence but added to fill out the meter, as in poetry, or to reveal the speaker's mood. For example, in the sentence, *Make it clear what you want*, the *it* is an expletive. So are exclamations such as *Damn!* or *Glory be!*

fricative | *n.* or *adj.* An unvoiced sound like *f-f-f* or *th-th-th* produced by air escaping through a constriction of the vocal passage, quieter and higher pitched than a **sibilant**.

gender | *n.* A category into which nouns, articles, pronouns, and adjectives are classified and in which there must be agreement. The genders are called masculine, feminine, and neuter, and these correspond to the sex of certain nouns. However, the gender of most nouns seems to depend on a perceived euphony with their articles. English is free of gender except for personal pronouns of the third person singular (and a handful of nouns) and these correspond to the sex of the subject. The genderless nature of English may explain why so few of us are multilingual and why English is the second language of so many.

gerund | *n.* The present participle of a verb used as a noun.

grammar | *n.* Originally, the elements and principles of any science or art. Now almost exclusively confined to the art and science of linguistics.

homonym | *n.* Sometimes confused with the word *homophone*. **Homonym** means *same name*, that is, *same meaning*, while **homophone** means *same sound*.

homophone | *n.* One of two or more words that differ in meaning but sound the same. *Sleigh* and *slay* are homophones, as are *rain, rein,* and *reign*.

hyphen | *n.* The "short bar" used to separate visually the syllable of a word, for example, *Con-stan-tin-o-ple,* and to tie together words closely related in a phrase, as in *jack-of-all-trades*. Also used to indicate the division of a word at the end of a line.

imperative (mode) | *adj.* The verb form used to express commands.

indicative (mode) | *adj.* The verb form used for most declarative and expository writing.

inflection | *n.* The change of form by which some words indicate certain grammatical relationships, as **number, case, gender, tense,** etc.

linking verbs (copulas) | *n.* A verb that serves to link its subject to other nouns, pronouns, or adjectives that follow it (in the predicate). This gives these words the same case (nominative) as the subject. Only the pronouns show this.

modifiers | *n.* Words that help characterize the words they modify—adjectives for nouns and pronouns, and adverbs for verbs, adjectives, and other adverbs.

nominative (case) | *adj.* The case called for in pronouns following a linking verb, as in: It is *I*.

number | *n.* A differentiation in grammatical form to show whether one or more than one is meant, that is, **singular** or **plural**.

object (of a verb) | *n.* The word that experiences the action described by the verb (direct object), or word(s) that tell to whom (or for what) the action took place (indirect object).

object (of a preposition) | *n.* The word that gives the temporal or spatial reference for the preposition.

objective (case) | *adj.* The case of words that are the object of verbs or prepositions. Visible only in pronouns.

paragraph | *n.* A group of one or more sentences that develops the thought expressed in the topic (initial) sentence.

participle | *n.* A verb form used as an adjective to describe the state of the subject, or used as a noun (see **gerund**). English verbs have two participles: the present, ending in *-ing*, and the past, ending in *-d, -ed, -en,* or *-n.* Example: a *running* brook, a *tired* boy.

parts of speech | *n.* The classic classes of words, depending on their function, for example, articles, nouns, verbs, adjectives, adverbs, pronouns, prepositions, conjunctions, and interjections.

passive (voice) | *adj.* The construction used to describe the action performed *upon* the subject by the verb. See **active**.

period | *n.* The single dot used to indicate the end of a sentence or an abbreviation.

phrase | *n.* A group of interacting words without a subject and predicate that together convey one of the elemental thoughts of the sentence. A phrase may serve as a part of speech.

plosive | *n.* A consonant in which the breath is suddenly released to form a rapid onset of sound, as in *b, p,* etc.

plural | *adj.* The word forms required when the subject or object consists of more than one person, place, or thing (the opposite of **singular**).

possessive (case) | *adj.* The case that indicates possession of or ownership by the noun in question, as in the *bird's* song, *our* house, etc.

predicate | *n.* The part of a sentence that says something about the subject. In normal sentence word order it is the verb (sometimes called the immediate predicate) and all that follows it.

predicate adjective | *n.* An adjective in the predicate that is linked by the verbs to its subject.

predicate nominative │ *n.* A noun or pronoun in the predicate that is linked by the verb to its subject and therefore has the same case (nominative).

preposition │ *n.* A word that tells the relation between two other words in a sentence—usually their relation in time or space, but often something more general, such as the degree of similarity. Thus *like* and *unlike* are prepositions.

principal parts (of a verb) │ *n.* By convention, these include the present and past first person singular, and the past participle of a verb. (Some writers choose the infinitive, present participle, past, and past participle.)

pronounce │ *v.* To speak the aural equivalent of a written letter, syllable, or word.

pronunciation │ *n.* The quality of one's oral reading, which depends upon the distinctness, clarity, and accent with which the words are spoken.

punctuation │ *n.* The separation of written text into sections, that is, paragraphs, by indenting and blocking; sentences, by initial capitals and final periods, exclamation, or questions marks; clauses by semicolons; and clauses, phrases, and appositives by commas. Punctuation is also used to indicate quotations and possessives.

reflexive │ *adj.* "Bent back on itself." Said of a sentence in which the object is also the subject. The reflexive pronouns all end in *-self.*

regular (case) │ *adj.* Belonging to one of the common classes of inflection.

restrictive (clause) │ *adj.* A clause that narrows the field of alternatives to be considered. Restrictive clauses are usually introduced by *that.*

semicolon │ *n.* The appropriate punctuation mark for the separation of independent clauses. Also used as a "supercomma" to separate items in a list when commas are used within each item.

sentence │ *n.* "A group of words expressing a complete thought" is the usual definition. "Complete" must not be taken to mean fully developed, or that nothing more need be said. Paragraphs answer more fully to that meaning. Rather, complete means coherent and self-consistent.

sibilant │ *n.* A consonant formed by the hissing of air through a small opening between the lips or tongue and teeth. The consonants *s, th, f,* and *sh* are sibilants.

singular │ *n.* The word forms used when there's only one subject or object (the opposite of **plural**).

spelling │ *n.* The translation of speech into a series of written symbols representing the successive sounds.

subject │ *n.* The noun or noun-phrase that either initiates the thought of the sentence or is central to it.

subjunctive (mode) │ *adj.* The construction and word forms used to express uncertainty among alternatives (present subjunctive) and as a statement contrary to fact (past subjunctive).

subordinate (clause) | *adj.* Of secondary importance or interest, relative to a primary or independent matter.

superlative (degree) | *adj.* The extreme form of an adjective, for example, *biggest, smallest, wisest, tallest.*

synonym | *n.* A word having a similar meaning to another word. The shades of difference that do exist make the choice important.

tense | *n.* The expression of time relations by a verb and its auxiliaries.

topic sentence | *n.* The initial and defining **sentence** of the subject of a paragraph.

usage | *n.* In language, the idiom, accent, and new meanings that characterize common practice.

voice | *n.* The term used to indicate whether A does something to B (active voice) or B has something done to it by A (passive voice). The same action is described but from two viewpoints. (See **active** and **passive**.)

voiced | *adj.* Sounds that are created using the vocal cords to produce all or part of the sound.

word | *n.* The smallest unit of speech to which meaning is attached.

(Note: Refer to the Index to locate those pages giving more in-depth descriptions of the terms above.)

REFERENCES

1. Smith, Langdon. "Evolution," reprinted in *The Best Loved Poems of the American People*. Edited by Hazel Felleman. Reissued ed. New York: Doubleday & Co., 1976.

2. White, E.B. *Writings from* The New Yorker, *1927–1976*. Edited by Rebecca Dale. New York: Harper Trade, 1991.

3. Fowler, H.W. *A Dictionary of Modern English Usage.* 2nd ed., revised by Ernest Gowers. New York: Oxford University Press, 1965.

4. Strunk, William Jr., and E.B. White. *The Elements of Style.* Revised ed. New York: Macmillan, 1959.

5. Phythian, B.A. *A Concise Dictionary of Confusables: All Those Impossible Words You Never Get Right.* New York: John Wiley & Sons, 1990.

6. Kilpatrick, James Jackson. *The Ear Is Human: A Handbook of Homophones and Other Confusions.* New York: Andrews, McNeel, Parker, 1985.

7. Berry, Thomas Elliott. *The Most Common Mistakes in English Usage.* New York: McGraw-Hill, 1971.

8. Warriner, John E. *English Composition and Grammar.* New York: Harcourt, Brace, Jovanovich, 1988.

9. Safire, William. *Coming to Terms.* New York: Henry Holt and Co., 1992.

Editor's Note: The books listed above were some of Barney's most-used references, and are cited throughout his own book. Because some of these publications may now be difficult to find, we have provided on the following two pages an additional list of selected bibliographical references. The books' tones range from serious and academic to light and entertaining, but every author is passionate about preserving the beauty of our language. We believe that Barney would have heartily approved of all.

SELECTED BIBLIOGRAPHY

Amis, Kingsley. *The King's English: A Guide to Modern Usage.* New York: St. Martin's Griffin, 1997.

Bernstein, Theodore M. *Do's, Don'ts & Maybes of English Usage.* New York: Gramercy Books, 1999.

Bernstein, Theodore M. *Miss Thistlebottom's Hobgoblins: The Careful Writer's Guide to the Taboos, Bugbears and Outmoded Rules of English Usage.* New York: The Noonday Press, 1991.

Burchfield, R.W. *The New Fowler's Modern English Usage.* Revised 3rd ed. New York: Oxford University Press, 2000.

Cazort, Douglas. *Under the Grammar Hammer: The 25 Most Important Grammar Mistakes and How to Avoid Them.* Los Angeles: Lowell House, 1997.

Fine, Edith H., and Judith P. Josephson. *Nitty-Gritty Grammar: A Not-So-Serious Guide to Clear Communication.* Berkeley: Ten Speed Press, 1998.

Follett, Wilson. *Modern American Usage: A Guide.* Revised by Erik Wensberg. New York: Hill and Wang, 1998.

Lederer, Richard, and Richard Dowis. *Sleeping Dogs Don't Lay*: Practical Advice for the Grammatically Challenged. *and that's no lie.* New York: St. Martin's Press, 1999.

Levin, Samuel R. *Shades of Meaning: Reflections on the Use, Misuse, and Abuse of English.* Boulder: Westview Press, 1998.

Lovinger, Paul W. *The Penguin Dictionary of American English Usage and Style.* New York: Penguin Reference, 2000.

O'Conner, Patricia T. *Woe Is I: The Grammarphobe's Guide to Better English in Plain English.* New York: Riverhead Books, 1996.

Partridge, Eric. *Usage and Abusage: A Guide to Good English*. Revised ed. Edited by Janet Whitcut. New York: W.W. Norton & Co., 1997.

Strunk, William Jr., and E.B. White. *The Elements of Style*. 4th ed. Boston: Allyn and Bacon, 2000.

Tarshis, Barry. *Grammar for Smart People: Your User-Friendly Guide to Speaking and Writing Better English*. New York: Pocket Books, 1992.

Wallraff, Barbara. *Word Court: Wherein Verbal Virtue Is Rewarded, Crimes Against the Language Are Punished, and Poetic Justice Is Done*. New York: Harcourt, Inc., 2000.

Walsh, Bill. *Lapsing Into a Comma: A Curmudgeon's Guide to the Many Things That Can Go Wrong in Print—and How to Avoid Them*. Chicago, IL: Contemporary Books, 2000.

Zinsser, William Knowlton. *On Writing Well: The Classic Guide to Writing Nonfiction*. Revised 6th ed. New York: Harper Reference, 1998.

DEDICATION

Not to be forgotten . . .

This book should fittingly be dedicated to the people who provided administrative support to Barney over the years and who often were the frontline soldiers in his battle for grammatical accuracy, conciseness, and challenging word usage. Reading Barney's handwriting itself was a formidable task, not because he was left-handed, but because his writing was extremely small. He used a soft-leaded drafting pencil and usually wrote very lightly on lined engineering pads or graph paper. As a result, he often had trouble reading his own hieroglyphics.

It was a challenge for a trained secretary or administrative assistant to function as a management team member with Barney. He preferred to answer his own phone (and anyone else's if he heard it ringing several times); he preferred to open his own mail (and to toss most of it, whether it needed further attention or not); and he maintained his own calendar (and was reluctant to keep his assistants informed about it, so he often missed appointments).

Yet, looking back, Barney's assistants view their days working for him as the best opportunity they had to stretch, to grow, to keep learning. His first and longtime HP secretary, Eileen Dugan, led the campaign years ago for Barney to write this "English Misusage" book. She knew that she and every HP employee who had been admonished by Barney was entitled to a copy, if for no other reason than to better understand the rules that had been broken.

Eileen probably expresses the sentiment of most of the people who worked for Barney in the touching tribute she sent to his children upon his death:

> *It was my good fortune to work by your father's side the better part (and I really do mean "better part") of thirty-one years. After seeing him in action day after day, I can attest to*

the enormous contributions he made to the company. On a personal basis, no one could have asked for a better boss, but he was more than a boss. He was a trusted friend, my mentor, whose diversity rubbed off on me and broadened my horizons. A man whose brilliance challenged me to learn, and to do the best that was in me just to keep in step with him, not to be found wanting. And while he may have caused me a headache or two along the way, he certainly never caused me to become bored! Many knew of his wit, his intelligence, his genius. I knew him for his kindness, his patience—yes, patience—and understanding, too. And, when trouble overtook our family now and again, no one could have asked for a more steadfast, generous friend. He was a rare man, a titan. We shall not see his like again soon.

During Barney's final years at HP, Rosemary Finnerty served as his secretary (for nearly ten years), and it was Rosemary who performed the Herculean task of producing the original drafts of this book, with additional help from Joanna Phillips. In the intervening HP years, various people provided administrative support, including Linda Ratcliff, Sherrie Shields, Judy Pollett, and others. No one was fonder of Barney than the NASA/SETI people who helped him maneuver through the cumbersome bureaucratic channels when Barney joined NASA in 1983, after retiring from HP. To Barney's great delight, both Elyse Murray and Chris Neller undertook production of Barney's technical papers on the computer by becoming T_eX experts! When Barney retired from NASA and joined the SETI Institute in 1994, Vera Buescher supported him as he led the drive for private funding to conduct the Institute's *Project Phoenix*, and Chris Neller continued to produce his technical papers.

Whether we say *lay* or *lie*, whether we ask that the document be sent to John and *me* or *I*, whether we use *which* rather than *that*, every one of us hears Barney's voice whispering the correct word or phrase in our ear, and we are each richer for it. Thank you, Barney.

VERA BUESCHER
Special Projects Coordinator
SETI Institute
Mountain View, California

SPECIAL TRIBUTE SECTION

Bernard M. Oliver

(1916–1995)

Bernard M. Oliver, Silicon Valley pioneer and director of research and development at Hewlett-Packard for three decades, died on November 23, 1995. He was seventy-nine years old.

A man of enormous intellect, curiosity, and vision, Dr. Oliver, known to his friends and family as Barney, leaves a legacy of extraordinary contributions in the fields of electronics, radio engineering, physics, astronomy, computer science, and biology.

Born in Soquel, California, Barney studied electrical engineering at Stanford University, graduating with a B.A. degree in 1935 at the age of nineteen. Two of his fellow students were William Hewlett and David Packard, both of whom were impressed by their precocious classmate. The following year, Barney earned an M.S. degree from the California Institute of Technology. He then spent a year studying in Germany on an exchange scholarship, returning to Caltech to complete his Ph.D., *magna cum laude,* in 1940. He was twenty-four years old.

Barney then joined the renowned Bell Telephone Laboratories in New Jersey, where he quickly established a reputation for brilliant, creative insights and clever inventions. He made major contributions to the development of the new and all-important "radar," and was a key contributor to the earliest television systems. His paper on pulse code modulation, *The Philosophy of PCM*, remains a seminal work to this day. While at Bell Labs, he met and married a young actress named Priscilla Newton, who was to share his life until she died in 1994. They had three children, Karen, Gretchen, and William Eric.

While Barney was making his mark at Bell Labs, William Hewlett and David Packard were starting a new electronics instrumentation firm in Palo Alto, California. They decided that Barney was the person they needed to lead their research efforts.

After many discussions and increasingly attractive offers, they persuaded Barney to join their fledgling operation. In 1952, Barney returned to his beloved California to become director of research for the Hewlett-Packard Company.

A hands-on director, Barney immediately set the standards of excellence that have become Hewlett-Packard's hallmark. In 1957, he became vice president of Research and Development, and in 1966, he established Hewlett-Packard Laboratories, the company's central research and development organization, which he directed until his retirement in 1981. Under Barney's leadership, HP Labs quickly became one of the world's foremost R&D organizations, as well as the birthplace of many of HP's most successful products, including the HP2116, HP's first computer; the HP9100 desktop programmable calculator; and the HP35, the first handheld calculator. Barney also served on the Hewlett-Packard Board of Directors from 1973 until 1981.

While at HP, Barney continued to pursue a lifelong interest in astronomy. His background in radio engineering prompted an interest in radio astronomy and the possibility that radio telescopes might be a means to detect extraterrestrial intelligent life. He was fascinated when, in 1960, attempts were made to detect radio waves from other civilizations. He had already calculated that such a search, with existing telescopes, made sense. He visited this first search at the National Radio Astronomy Observatory in Green Bank, West Virginia, but it was not until 1971 that he was able to fully immerse himself in this endeavor. Taking time off from HP, Barney guided a major feasibility study of possible radio telescope systems for the search for extraterrestrial intelligence (SETI), sponsored by Stanford University and the NASA Ames Research Center.

This effort spawned *Project Cyclops*, a seminal and grandiose plan for a radio telescope system capable of detecting quite ordinary extraterrestrial radio signals from great distances in our galaxy. Although the design was very sound and the report a monument to fine scientific and technical writing, the projected ultimate cost of the project, some tens of billions of dollars, far exceeded what was politically acceptable. The report stands to this day as a sound description of an ingenious and noble, albeit unfulfilled, enterprise.

Barney retained a close relationship to SETI throughout the rest of his life. He made numerous contributions to the scientific and technical design of SETI searches and systems. Following his retirement from HP, Barney devoted his energies full time to SETI, serving as director of the NASA Ames SETI office from 1982 to 1993. During this period, SETI became a major project within NASA, with an overall budget of more than $100 million. This project reached a milestone in the fall of 1992, when its extremely sophisticated radio receiving equipment started searching for extraterrestrial radio signals at both the Goldstone tracking station of NASA and the Arecibo Observatory in Puerto Rico. Unfortunately, the U.S. Congress cut off funding for this project just one year after the searching began.

Some ten years earlier, Barney had been a prime mover in the formation of the SETI Institute, a not-for-profit scientific institute that was formed to conduct research related to life in the universe with maximum efficiency and at the lowest possible cost. Disdaining bureaucracy and waste, Barney saw the SETI Institute as an experiment that would demonstrate that the highest quality research could be done with minimal management and overhead costs. Upon his retirement from NASA in January 1994, he joined the Board of Directors of the Institute. Over the decade since its inception, the Institute has become an extremely successful research center, just as Barney imagined and planned it would. His last act for the Institute was to provide it with a major bequest to ensure its continued activity and success for a very long time.

Barney received a host of awards during his life, foremost of which is the National Medal of Science, which he received at the White House in 1986. He served as vice president (1962) and president (1965) of the Institute of Electrical and Electronic Engineers (IEEE), after being made a Fellow of its predecessor, the Institute of Radio Engineers, in 1954 and director-at-large in 1958.

In 1966, he was appointed to the President's Commission on the Patent System. In 1990, he received both NASA's Medal for Exceptional Engineering and the Pioneer Award of the International Foundation for Telemetering in recognition of a lifetime of service to the telecommunications profession.

Other significant honors include the Caltech Distinguished Alumnus Award for 1972; IEEE's Lamme Medal for meritorious achievement in the development of electronic instrumentation and measuring devices, 1977; the Halley Lectureship on Astronomy and Terrestrial Magnetism of Oxford University, 1984; and the Harvey Mudd College Wright Prize for Multidisciplinary Scientific or Engineering Accomplishments, 1984. He was Adjunct Professor of Astronomy at the University of California, Berkeley, and served on the Boards of Directors of the Exploratorium in San Francisco, Geostar Corporation, and Associated Universities, Inc. He was a founder of the Biosys Corporation, which seeks environmentally sound means to eliminate agricultural pests.

Barney was awarded some 60 patents, and he authored some 71 publications in more than seven scientific and technical fields. In 1991, Hewlett-Packard Laboratories established the "Bernard M. Oliver Symposium on the Future," an annual distinguished lecture series in his honor. He received the NASA Group Achievement Award for the NASA SETI project in 1993.

Barney also generously donated his time in the service of education and the community. He served on the Palo Alto Unified School District Board from 1961 to 1971, and was a member of the Engineering Advisory Councils at both Stanford and the University of California, Berkeley. He was appointed for ten years as a consultant on the engineering and safety of the new San Francisco/Oakland Bay Area Rapid Transit (BART) System. He served as a consultant to the Army Scientific Advisory Panel, and was a member of the Congressional Review Committee for the National Bureau of Standards. Just before his death, Barney was an active member of the Dean's Advisory Council for Natural Sciences at the University of California, Santa Cruz.

He was a generous donor to causes he felt were important, although he never sought public recognition for his philanthropy. He made major contributions to the universities he had attended, as well as to the Universities of California at Berkeley and Santa Cruz. At Santa Cruz he endowed a scholarship fund in Theater Arts in honor of his wife, Priscilla Newton. He contributed to many educational enterprises, including contributions of computers and associated equipment to middle schools.

Barney especially liked to support scientific enterprises he deemed worthy but, in some cases, neglected, especially if they might contribute to understanding and discovery of life in the universe. He made major contributions to the Exploratorium, the Monterey Bay Aquarium, and the San Francisco State University/Marine World Dolphin Communications Project. Among his largest gifts was one to the Allegheny Observatory at the University of Pittsburgh to allow the upgrading of the lens of its largest telescope, which was being used to search for extrasolar planetary systems. Another was a $200,000 challenge grant to the Monterey Institute for Research in Astronomy (MIRA), which used the funds to build a high-quality observatory at Chew's Ridge, near Carmel, which was named the "Oliver Station" in honor of Barney.

Barney was widely known and admired for his strong communication skills, a trait Barney attributed to his mother, a teacher who instilled in him at an early age a reverence for proper grammar. As a result, his scientific papers were models of clarity, his conversations terse and to the point. In short, he believed that clear, concise communication was important to success, whether the communication be with humans, dolphins, or people of other stars. As one final bequest to humanity, just before he died, Barney finished the manuscript of this book detailing the fine points of English grammar and why they, in fact, ensure clarity in communication.

Barney Oliver's cornucopia of intellectual and practical gifts to the world, as well as his personal example, will continue to enrich us far into the future.

Young Barney, who went to school at age 4 with his mother, the teacher.

Such a serious look; possibly Barney was already thinking about waveguides or the laws of physics as a young student.

Barney Oliver accepted Bill Hewlett and Dave Packard's invitation to join Hewlett-Packard in 1952 as head of Research and Development. (HP Photo, 1973)

Bill Hewlett and Barney Oliver look on as Lee de Forest tries out a new HP waveguide device during a tour of HP in 1956.

Barney Oliver in his favorite mode— with sleeves rolled up, in the engineering lab, sorting out an intriguing problem with Peter Lacy and George Mathers. (HP Photo, mid-1950s)

Barney Oliver proudly presenting the new HP9100 Calculator, whose birth he led in the mid- to late-1960s.

Barney was always ready to explore a new idea or ask penetrating questions about a new experiment.

Barney's wit and humor are legendary—he strikes an interesting pose with Sebastian von Hoerner at Green Bank, West Virginia, in 1984.

"Would you buy a used car from this guy? John Billingham answers, "Yes. It would be in better condition than when it was new." John should know: he now drives the last car Barney owned.

PERSONAL TRIBUTES TO BARNEY OLIVER

MODERN ENGLISH MISUSAGE

SPECIAL MEMORIAL EDITION

OVERVIEW

THREE FORMER BOSSES SPEAK . . .

Barney often boasted that he never worked a day in his life. He liked and respected the people he worked for throughout his career. He loved solving complex problems, so he enjoyed each challenging day and didn't look upon it as work. No one was affected more by Barney's death than three former bosses for whom he worked so loyally. For more than 40 years, Barney served as head of Research and Development at Hewlett-Packard, working for and with two remarkable friends—now legendary techno-giants—whom he'd met as fellow Stanford students, David Packard and William Hewlett. Barney was also passionate about SETI, and that led him to eventually accept John Billingham's invitation to head the SETI Program at NASA's Ames Research Center. It is truly fitting that we open this special section (see pages 108–111) with tributes by these three special people whom Barney held in such high regard. These people are:

David Packard, Hewlett-Packard Co.
William Hewlett, Hewlett-Packard Co.
John Billingham, SETI Institute

"BARNEY" SPEAKS . . .

At Barney's memorial service, Jill Tarter of the SETI Institute presented a collection of quotes from Barney, which provided a flavor of his diversity in interests, in patience, and in passion. Jill held Barney in the highest regard, and he, her. Barney would heartily approve of the SETI Institute's decision to name Jill as the first holder of the Bernard M. Oliver Chair for the Search for Extraterrestrial Intelligence. Jill's tribute touched everyone at Barney's memorial service. It was as though he were speaking directly to each person. Thanks to Jill's creativity, we have this opportunity to listen to Barney once again. (See pages 112–116.)

Jill Tarter, SETI Institute

FAMILY, FRIENDS, AND COLLEAGUES SPEAK . . .

Barney would have been amazed at the number of tributes from all facets of his life that flowed in after his death. Reading the selected excerpts that follow on pages 117–160, one is struck by the reach of Barney's footprint around the globe. We ask your consideration for the editor's selections; it was impossible to include all the contributed texts in their entirety in this book. It's fun to imagine what Barney would say were he reading these frank, heartfelt recollections himself.

A NOTED SCIENCE FICTION AUTHOR
Sir Arthur C. Clarke

BELL LABS
Chapin Cutler
John Pierce

HEWLETT-PACKARD CO.
Joel Birnbaum
Al Bagley
Frank Carrubba
Frank Cavier
Bob Conley

HEWLETT-PACKARD CO. (cont.)
Len Cutler
Zvonko Fazarinc
Rosmary E. Finnerty
Don Hammond
Emery Rogers
Dave Yewell

NASA
Daniel S. Goldin
Hans Mark
Geoff Briggs
Gary Coulter
Lynn Harper
Angelo Gustaferro

SETI INSTITUTE
Frank Drake
Tom Pierson
Vera Buescher
Kent Cullers
Edna DeVore
Laurance Doyle
Chris Neller
Alan Patrick
Charles Seeger
Seth Shostak
Jill Tarter

COLLEAGUES IN THE UNITED STATES
Britton Chance
Tom Clark
Nathan Cohen
Leonard David
George Gatewood
R. Dwayne Highfill
John G. Linvill
Karl S. Pister
Stan Runyon
David Soderblom

SETI AROUND THE WORLD

Puerto Rico
Tom Hagfors
Mike Davis

United States
Robert Dixon
Louis Friedman
Paul Horowitz
Stuart A. Kingsley
H. Paul Shuch
Jack Welch
Dan Werthimer

Australia
John Brooks
Carol Oliver
Bobbie Vaile
Kelvin Wellington

Canada
Dale Russell

Russia
Nikolay S. Kardashev
Vladimir Strelnitski

PERSONAL FRIENDS AND ASSOCIATES
Bob Asquith
Reed Larson
Dick Madigan
Mick Ruthven
Fred and Nelda Warren
Eric P. Wente
Robert B. Yonts, Jr.

FAMILY
William Eric Oliver
Gretchen More Oliver
Karen Newton Oliver

THREE FORMER BOSSES SPEAK . . .

 Brilliant Scientist, Great Human Being

I first met Barney Oliver 62 years ago. In the fall quarter of my senior year at Stanford, I enrolled in Professor Terman's graduate course called "Radio Engineering." I was the first undergraduate allowed to take this course. A junior from Caltech enrolled at Stanford at the same time. He asked Fred Terman if he could also take his radio engineering class, and Professor Terman allowed him to do so with the stipulation that if he failed in the first mid-quarter examination he would have to drop out. Barney not only had the highest grade in that examination, he also got the highest grade in the class in every examination that year!

In the spring of 1934, all the engineering students at Stanford began to worry about finding a job when they graduated. Bill Hewlett, Ed Porter, and I decided that we would form our own company if we did not find satisfactory jobs, and Barney Oliver agreed to join us. It turned out that I received a job offer from the General Electric Company in Schenectady, New York. Professor Terman advised me to take that job because I would learn many things there that would be helpful when we eventually started our own company. He said that Bill Hewlett would benefit from several years of graduate work. After graduating, Barney took a job at the Bell Telephone Laboratories, where he did some pioneering work with John Pierce on information theory. When the United States became involved in World War II, he shifted his work to radar.

Bill Hewlett and I convinced him to join us at HP in 1952.

Barney was not only a brilliant scientist, but also a great human. I have never known anyone who did not like Barney. He also had a great sense of humor. On one occasion, Art Fong, one of our Chinese engineers, asked Barney to give him an evaluation on whether the project Art was working on would succeed. Barney's response was, "It does not have a Chinaman's chance!"

This statement from one of our HP employees sums up what everyone thought of Barney:

"It is one of the saddest tasks I have ever undertaken to inform you that this Thanksgiving evening, our dear friend, mentor, colleague, and my boss, Barney Oliver, died of a heart attack. Barney was a good friend to a lot of people. I learned to admire and respect him during my nine years working with him. He was very generous, caring, and always had time to chat if you came by his office."

After 62 years of working with Barney Oliver, I consider him not only one of the best scientists I have ever known, but also one of the best friends I ever had.

DAVID PACKARD (1912–1996)
Co-Founder, Hewlett-Packard Co.
Palo Alto, California

 ## A Wonderful Role Model

I am not sure where I first met Bernard M. Oliver—"Barney" to all of us. It must have been during my early years at Stanford. After he graduated from Caltech and Stanford, Barney went to work at Bell Labs. Whenever I went back East, I always tried to visit him, as I was impressed with his abilities and felt he would be a major addition to the Hewlett-Packard Company.

I recall that when Barney was at Stanford, Professor Terman was going to teach a senior level course in radio engineering (electronics now). Barney was interested in taking the course, but Terman was doubtful because at that time, Barney was only a junior. However, Barney insisted and Professor Terman relented, telling him, "Fine. We'll see how you do in the midterms." The midterms came up and Barney got the highest grade in the class.

As I said, I always kept track of Barney. Initially, when Dave and I planned to start our company in the late 1930s, we asked Barney if he would join us. However, he was happy with his work at Bell Labs and turned us down. Years later, the circumstances changed for Barney, and he wanted to come west, so he agreed to join us. That was about 1952.

He was appointed director of research at Hewlett-Packard and elected vice president and member of the board of directors. When HP Labs was set up, he headed that.

At the time, we were allocating 10 percent of our net income to the manufacturing divisions to carry on their own development programs. This turned out to be too narrow a spectrum of research, however, and we set up HP Labs. Its charter was quite broad. The funds allocated to the Labs were approximately 1 percent of net income, and they could freelance in whatever area they saw fit. Sometimes they chose to help a manufacturing division increase their research program.

Occasionally the Labs started programs of their own in a promising field, which subsequently proved interesting and was eventually transferred to one of the manufacturing divisions. Thus, between the Labs and the manufacturing divisions, we covered a fairly broad spectrum of activities.

I remember at one of the annual management meetings, Barney presented an enthusiastic description of an outside inventor: Tom Osborne. His invention involved a simplified computer structure. This subsequently turned into the 9100 project, one of the most successful ventures in the field of computers. This gave me an opportunity to observe Barney as a mathematician, a surveyor, an astronomer, a salesman, and an accomplished repair technician!

Barney was also a wonderful role model of how to apply logic to practical problems. An example was Barney's help with our first minicomputer. We had it all designed and the specifications set, only to discover there was no room for the power supply in the model. This was exactly the kind of problem Barney loved, and right then and there he invented a different kind of power supply—much lighter and smaller—that would fit into the space available.

Not only did he teach the engineering staff technical matters, but he also taught them how to speak the King's English. I learned firsthand that "data" was a plural noun, not singular. Without hesitation Barney pointed out my error—and I never forgot it!

Barney's interests were so catholic that it was hard to constrain them. For instance, he was fascinated by astronomy—which led to the current SETI program (the Search for Extraterrestrial Intelligence).

He also became interested in the use of an ordinary garden pest for controlling troublesome insects. His scheme was to develop a strain of nematodes, which were insectivorous. With the help of HP, he set up a company to produce these nematodes. It turned out that they had limited value, although important in some cases. Although we subsequently backed out of this, it is an example of Barney's breadth of interests.

Barney left an indelible mark on the company. He will always be recognized as the great genius that he really was.

WILLIAM HEWLETT (1913–2001)
Co-Founder, Hewlett-Packard Co.
Palo Alto, California

⭐ An Amazing Story

Barney was my mentor and friend for 25 years. I consider it the greatest honor to have been able to work closely with him through those years. We both considered SETI to be one of the most important challenges and opportunities of all time. I remember so well meeting with him at the Palo Alto Club in the fall of 1970 to invite him to direct the first comprehensive engineering design study of a system for detecting extraterrestrial intelligent life. He said he would have to check with Dave and Bill. Then he signed on. Two years later, mostly as a result of his extraordinary technical genius, his report was published as *Project Cyclops*. I was amazed, and so was everyone who read it (except for a few bureaucrats, who didn't read it, but just grumbled about the cost). It was a masterpiece, and became recognized as such. It enabled SETI to gain acceptance as a bona fide scientific and engineering enterprise, and allowed the NASA SETI program to get under way. It would not have happened without him.

The next amazing thing that Barney did was to accept my invitation to join NASA and head the SETI program at the Ames Research Center. It is fair to say that Barney was not enamored of bureaucracies, but here he was, becoming a civil servant. As he said himself, he was not a servant, and certainly not civil. It was the magic of SETI that did it. In turn, he made SETI what it became, the most imaginative of all NASA's enterprises. In the fullness of time, a real system was built and a real search inaugurated. In the halcyon days of October 1992, Barney was there at Arecibo Observatory in Puerto Rico to see an early stage of his vision become reality. He gave us an amazing speech, revealing again his command, not only of technical matters, but of the English language.

In recent years, he has been a rock of intellectual stability for all of us at the SETI Institute, where *Project Phoenix* continues the search with private funding from generous donors, including Barney himself.

Coming from England, I used to think that my own command of the English language was somewhat superior. After being exposed to Barney for a year or two, I revised that opinion. In fact, he corrected my grammar and syntax just as he did with everyone else. But now, after 25 years of learning from the master, I feel superior again. So I solemnly pledge to carry the torch and correct everyone's English. He would not have wanted it any other way.

I really miss him.

JOHN BILLINGHAM
Former NASA SETI Program Chief
Volunteer—Senior Scientist, SETI Institute
Mountain View, California

"Barney" Speaks . . .

 ### Jill Tarter Shares Selected Excerpts from Barney in His Own Words

Oh, how Barney could write; with grammatical precision, accuracy, attention to detail, sarcasm, wit, and great vision. So, I'd like to allow Barney to speak for himself by quoting fragments from his papers and correspondence over the past years on a wide range of topics that occupied his ever-curious mind.

I only learned about Barney in the post-Cyclops era. In 1971, Barney took a leave from HP to direct, write, edit, and publish the *Project Cyclops* report. This report was the single most successful combination of recruiting document and communication theory text I have yet encountered. As we know, one of the things Barney believed in passionately was SETI. This quote eloquently explains why.

Barney, on the reason for doing SETI:

To me SETI is a search for proof that natural selection and evolution are ubiquitous and that they frequently lead to beings as complicated as humans. We SETI buffs are enthralled by the knowledge that on this little planet the wonderful laws of physics have, in a few billion years, converted the ravening chaos of the Big Bang into the most delicate and complex of structures—into spiderwebs and apple blossoms and leaping trout, and above all into brains capable of modeling the exterior world and puzzling out its origin. We want to know if this astonishing transformation is a local freak event or an inherent property of the universe. We very much suspect the latter.

Although Barney was a big fan of science fiction, for him it was just that, *fiction*. He refused to project into the future those things that violated our current understanding of physics or his own notion of common sense. This was not always a popular stand.

Barney, on interstellar travel:

Paradoxically, the universe is so big that life can be at once both abundant and sparse. Even the nearest star is so distant that a one-hundred-percent efficient rocket, to make the round trip in a human lifetime, would need all the energy the world consumes in over three centuries. With such a price tag, many of us feel that interstellar travel is and will remain the science fiction writer's dream.

. . . you used the words ". . . until that inevitable day when we venture out to the stars."

When I was a kid I thought it was inevitable too and could hardly wait until the state-of-the-art caught up with my dreams. But along the way I studied the teachings of Sir Isaac Newton and Albert Einstein and now can no longer believe in the old-time inevitability. Nature does not deny us the stars, exactly, but sets a price so high that I am afraid I am no longer interested.

. . . we did not say that interstellar travel is "completely" impossible; we said it was economically forbidden. There's a big difference. We agree it can be done, but we also insist that the price is too high.

Barney loved rockets, but he also loved nature and tried hard to make its workings understandable to anyone.

BARNEY, ON THE MOON AND SUN:

Some clear night, when the Moon is at first quarter, try to see it, not as a semicircle, but as the full sphere it really is, side-lighted by the now hidden Sun. Remember that you are looking at dark lava and regolith. If some giant graffiti artist were to spray the Moon pure white it would be almost 15 times brighter—as bright as a white cloud on a sunny day. Now think of all the light that misses the Earth and Moon and sweeps past us into the depths of space. This spill is enough to warm over two billion Earths, for we cover less than half a billionth of the Sun's sky.

Barney loved mathematics for its own sake, not just as an essential tool for engineers and scientists. He reserved the right to do his mathematics in whatever units were best suited to the job.

BARNEY, ON METRICATION:

The United States became the leader in world trade under the English system long before there was any talk of metrication. We lost that leadership not because we failed to metrify, but because we became fat, dumb, and critical of our own affluence. . . . We will regain leadership if and when we are willing to work harder and honor our own country's prophets. Using centimeters has nothing to do with it. I don't see Canada surging ahead because they've gone metric. Of course, they've gone bilingual as well, which really slows things down.

. . . I use the metric system a lot; I do so when I feel it is appropriate. But I don't want to be legislated into having to use it all the time.

. . . One thing seems certain. You will diminish the already pathetic ability of the scientist to dramatize the grandeur of science. Tell me that a supernova releases 10^{51} ergs and I

yawn. But tell me that in its fiery death it outshines a galaxy of 100 billion stars and I come alive.

Comets and asteroids are the only bodies in the skies that can be named after people. Right now, orbiting the Sun every 5.7 years is "Asteroid Oliver," named so by Barney's friends as a tribute to his interest in detecting Earth-crossing asteroids soon enough to avoid any possible collisions.

BARNEY, ON SPACEWATCH:

I enjoyed the opportunity to discuss Project Spacewatch with you. I am delighted to learn that there has been a revival of interest in this project. I would like to believe that my species had the foresight to avoid the sort of catastrophe that wiped out the dinosaurs and that NASA had the courage to lead the way in developing our defense. I cannot think of a more appropriate long-term role for the agency than the defense of all intelligent life on Earth.

Over the years, Barney lectured to, interacted with, and was acted upon by the U.S. Congress. It isn't too hard to imagine his thoughts on that subject.

BARNEY, ON CONGRESS:

In times when reductions in government spending are being sought, the temptation to turn down any new program, regardless of its merits, is very strong. The way to make real budget reductions is to cut out large and old programs that have proven to be ineffective or that have outlived their usefulness, and to balance the remaining programs, not to practice infanticide. . . . It takes real courage to stand up in Congress and say that a program is ineffective, that the jobs it provides are unproductive. But don't we have a right to expect courage in our representatives? (Written in 1979!)

The SETI office has always gotten its share of crank mail. It's amazing that Barney often took the time to try to educate the letter writers.

BARNEY, ON PSEUDOSCIENCE:

As a resident of this country, I have been aware of the UFO hysteria for the last 40 years. At first the reported sightings attracted my interest but, as time went on and sincere investigation failed to produce any hard evidence for their existence, I am afraid my interest faded. Now, when asked if I believe in UFOs, I say, "Certainly, I've seen lots of flying objects I couldn't identify. I just don't happen to believe they are of extraterrestrial origin."

Barney's early educational experience shaped his lifelong approach to learning, and it was intimately connected with his mother, Margaret. She was drafted into teaching when Barney was four years old, so he went to school every day with her.

BARNEY, ON HIS MOTHER, MARGARET:

I recall sitting on the bench at recitation time and crying out "ab, eb, ib, ob, ub" in unison with the huge first graders on either side of me. Together we learned our phonics and our fractions. I learned to read and write while mother learned to teach reading and writing. . . .

As a teacher, Margaret was always master of her classroom. . . . She did not seek a well-rounded child, she stretched them as far as they could stretch. She was the teacher youngsters remember, the teacher who actually taught.

Barney also taught—his was a lesson in courage as he cared for his wife, Suki, in her final years.

BARNEY, ON SUKI AS A CHILD:

When life at home seemed intolerable to the aspiring young lady, she would sometimes leave to seek her fame and fortune, only to be rescued a few hours later as far south as the neighboring town of Shelburne. In her suitcase were only her dancing costume and shoes.

BARNEY, ON SUKI'S DYING:

Dear Sebastian:

. . . I wish the best for you and Lisa. I am OK still, but Suki, with her Alzheimer's is slowly going downhill. It's a hard way to lose her.

Barney could write about himself as candidly and as pointedly as he did about others.

BARNEY, ON BARNEY:

I was fascinated with radio, which was new when I was new. My father built one of the first radio receivers in California. . . . I remember once sitting up in the wee hours of the morning and tuning in a faint squeal.

In general, I have not contented myself with learning in isolated disciplines, but I've tried to integrate everything together. In other words, I refuse to hold what I consider to be mutually conflicting views. If I believe one thing, and another belief is impossible because of that, I have to choose between them. I have tried to find the way the world works.

Retirement, ugh!. . . I have no intention of vegetating. I find it more interesting to live a life full of endeavor and working towards things I believe in.

STASIS AT SUNSET
(presented by Barney to Charles Seeger on his 70th birthday)

You barely outpace us, Sun in our flight
As Westward we jet, postponing night.
Suspended in time, suspended in space,
Conestoga clouds drift past your face.
Which is more real O King of the Sky,
Those phantom wagons, or subsonic I?

I have been extraordinarily fortunate to be able, from an early age, to know, and work with, and argue with such a giant of a man! When one begins a career by standing on the shoulders of a giant such as Barney, one has the luxury of daring anything and embracing the seemingly impossible. From a perch atop those giant shoulders, many obstacles can be overlooked and one's vision can be unlimited. For those of us working in SETI, Barney's shoulders are no longer here to support us. So our team must replace them with a scaffolding built of the lessons we have learned from him and the values he has instilled. We must make that scaffolding strong with determination and with intellectual integrity. From this new support platform each of us must stretch higher and reach farther than we personally thought we could in order to continue extending the vision that Barney inspired, until we eventually achieve the seemingly impossible. To do less would diminish the memory of those wonderful, giant shoulders that labored so hard, for so long, to support the next generation who would shape the future.

This will be no easy task, given our sadness. We all miss him. However, this giant has left to each of us a piece of himself—there can be no better tool than that for getting on with the job!

JILL TARTER
Director, SETI Programs
SETI Institute
Mountain View, California

FAMILY, FRIENDS, AND COLLEAGUES SPEAK . . .

 ### A Noted Science Fiction Author

I'm indeed saddened to hear of Barney Oliver's death. How I wish he could have lived long enough to see the SETI programme, to which he contributed so much, crowned with success.

I have particularly happy memories of Barney, as I was once privileged to be his house guest. He (and Bill Hewlett) were responsible for presenting me with my first desktop calculator, the HP9100A, a quarter of a century ago. "Hal Junior"—still working perfectly—is now in the computer museum of the Arthur Clarke Centre here in Colombo. Later, Barney gave me one of the first HP35s—the ancestor of all the millions of today's pocket computers.

I send my sympathy to his family, and I hope that his example will continue to provide inspiration to engineers and scientists for a long time to come.

SIR ARTHUR C. CLARKE, CBE
Chancellor, International Space University
Chancellor, University of Moratuwa
Sri Lanka

⭐ Bell Labs

When I joined Bell Telephone Laboratories in 1937, one of the first things I learned was that "When Barney comes, things will be different." I was thrown into the company of four remarkable engineer-scientists who had emerged from Caltech the year before: John Pierce, Dean Woodridge, Chuck Elmendorf, and Jim (Mac) McRae. I remember wondering what kind of person could earn the respect, almost awe, that these guys expressed.

Two years later, Barney arrived from Caltech, and I found out. He did make a difference. He had strong feelings on any subject that came to his attention, and amazing powers of expression. I don't recall ever winning an argument with him, and I seldom had the courage to try.

Just following WWII, our management created a committee of four of us who apparently were perceived as leaders in the younger generation of technical staff. Barney, Warren Tyrrell, Win Kick, and I were assigned the task of examining and evaluating the organizational habits and practices used among those involved in device-oriented research in Bell Labs. We were given carte blanche to examine anything and to interview anyone, and we did. We talked with the inventors of the coaxial line, waveguide, electronic feedback, the Hartley Oscillator, the radio altimeter, the transistor, the Pierce electron gun, and the Nyquist Theorem. We interviewed our technical aides and our bosses.

We talked with everyone whose opinion we respected, digested their wisdom, and wrote our own opinions in a report for our managers. Barney was incisive. He was intrepid. He was merciless. His ability to elicit answers and then transform them into clear writing was impressive. He had no patience for nonsense and less for incompetence. Had he been less competent himself, he would have made lots of enemies, but he was right so often that he accumulated more admirers than enemies.

The committee draft report was acknowledged and promptly buried. Yes, some of the recommendations were carried out in due course, and all four of us prospered in Bell Labs. Too soon Barney left for HP, but he continued for many years to be a very effective conduit between Bell Labs research and the HP laboratories, advancing technology in both organizations and still influencing Bell Labs.

I continue to be in awe of the man.

CHAPIN CUTLER
Former colleague at Bell Labs
Professor Emeritus
Stanford University

Twenty-two percent of Barney's active technical career was spent at Bell Labs. That's measuring from 1940, when he went to the Labs, to the very last days of his life. There was no stopping him once he got started.

Forty-four percent of Barney's 45 earlier patents belong to his Bell Labs years. That's a lot. I know that Bell Labs encouraged patenting, so as to have patents to trade with. But 20 patents in 12 years is a lot. Barney was very inventive at the Labs.

During the war, Barney worked on radar, and after the war he worked on the development of sophisticated TV reception. In 1948, Barney, Claude Shannon, and I published a paper, *The Philosophy of PCM*. We believed that the future of communications lay with digital encoding and processing. It certainly did.

Barney knew many Bell Labs people well. He and I shared a deep admiration for Harald Friis. Spending an hour with Harald and one or two of his people was the best way of tackling technical problems by talking technical sense. For years after Harald's retirement from Bell Labs, Barney had Harald come to HP to sit down with young researchers. Barney wrote briefly and movingly of Harald and his gift after Harald's death.

I feel that I knew Barney so very, very well when he was at Bell Labs, and ever after. Now I want to say, "Barney, how was it that so and so did so and so. . . ?" It's too late. Too late to ask Barney's help once more. But not too late to cherish and miss him.

JOHN PIERCE
Former colleague at Bell Labs
Visiting Professor Emeritus
Stanford University

Hewlett-Packard Company

Barney's life and career had a deep impact on all of Hewlett-Packard and on our community, in fact, on much of the country. Barney was the first and founding director of HP Labs, and was its technical spirit, its technical leader, and its organizational head until he retired from HP in 1981.

Barney insisted on getting things right, both what we did and how we described it. I think the reason that all of us could accept both grammatical corrections and criticisms of our work from Barney was that we knew that underneath it all lay this towering intelligence that was trying to drive us to do the very best we could. He made no fewer demands on himself than he did on us. The spirit of Barney continues to stalk the halls and the corridors at HP. He demanded technical contribution, not just technical participation. He inspired our risk-taking. It's Barney's most precious legacy to us, and we promise to guard it well.

JOEL BIRNBAUM
Senior Vice President, R&D
Director of HP Laboratories
Palo Alto, California

Among other attributes, Barney should be remembered for bravery. When he joined Hewlett-Packard, he saw that we had already done some pretty good engineering, but he knew that the average could be improved. He agreed that we should be proud when one of our ideas worked, but he thought that if we understood *why* it worked, we could probably take it even farther. So he started presenting a series of lectures on circuit theory, physics, and some advanced mathematics that he thought appropriate. It is true that Barney's persistent efforts changed H-and-P from Hunt and Peck engineering into a company with a worldwide reputation for scientific contribution. HP engineers grew to understand and appreciate the depth of his contribution.

Barney's focus wasn't just on the technical side. We all know what a stickler he was about the spoken word. His children recently reminded me that among Barney's most deserved awards was a very special one—a "Black Belt in English Grammar."

AL BAGLEY
Manager, Santa Clara Division
Hewlett-Packard (retired)
Palo Alto, California

During the past four years, since leaving Hewlett-Packard, I've often thought of Barney Oliver. His numerous contributions to science and engineering and to the Hewlett-Packard Company will be valued and remembered for many years to come.

I have benefited from Barney's wisdom and guidance. I will remember him as a man uncompromising in his pursuit of excellence and sensitive to events and people who touched his life in a special way.

There were times when Barney would make my blood boil with frustration, and only later would I realize that what he was telling me was, for the most part, true. His clear and refreshing views on particular topics often opened my mind and broadened my views.

I, like many others who knew and worked with Barney Oliver, will miss his manner, his deep and broad knowledge of science and engineering, and his view of the world in which he lived, not to mention the vast universe that served as his playground in recent years. I am certain Barney now knows the answers to the questions he was asking.

Frank Carrubba
Former Director of HP Laboratories
Palo Alto, California

Barney the fisherman! In the early 1950s, a group of fellows from Hewlett-Packard started going on trout fishing trips together every summer. Most of these fellows were from the Machine Shop and Assembly areas of the plant, a real blue-collar bunch, and you might think that Barney wouldn't be interested in spending a week each year with such a group. But Barney heard about all the fun we had, and in 1966 he hinted that he would like to join us. On hearing that, I asked, "Barney? Barney Oliver? Going fishing? Has he ever been out of doors?" Well, his 50th birthday was approaching, so as a birthday present we gave him the fishing equipment he would need, and took him fishing with us. He never missed a fishing trip for the next 29 years!

We know that Barney loved to correct our grammar. Any misuse of a word or phrase would be called to our attention, and Barney would give us the correct version. One of our gang, Jack Goodwin, was describing to all of us some event he had witnessed and he said, "When I walked in, this guy was laying on the floor." At which Barney said, "That's lying, Jack." Jack replied, "No, by God, it's the truth. I was there and I saw it; he was just laying there!"

Barney learned to play cribbage on his first fishing trip, and soon became an expert. There are endless stories to be told. He was our master chef, and we ate like kings. Barney loved those fishing trips. He loved the fishing, he loved the cribbage games and the camaraderie. He loved our gang and we love him. But all good things must come to an end, and there's nothing we can do about it except to cherish his memory.

FRANK CAVIER
Vice President of Finance
Hewlett-Packard (retired)
Palo Alto, California

Very few of us at Spokane Division had ever met Barney, including me, as HP had become such a large company and many of us were just starting our HP careers at the time of Barney's retirement. I think "Lost Opportunity" characterizes our regrets, as we were so close to meeting him and exploring the Coeur d'Alene area together as he was scheduled to speak at our next Division meeting on February 6, 1996.

One of the last things that Barney said to me as he was scheduling his presentation was, "You know, Bob, I'm an old man and I could be heading for the hospital on the Friday before your conference." Was he always so matter-of-fact?

Again, let me offer our deepest sympathy for the loss of your friend, a legend, and a great explorer.

BOB CONLEY
Hewlett-Packard, Spokane Division
Liberty Lake, Washington

Barney had the ability to see very quickly the crucial and important aspects of a situation or project, and knew exactly the right questions to ask to point out where there were weaknesses or additional work that needed to be done. He could sit in a project review and sometimes would fall asleep, but at the right time would wake up and ask the critical question or make an ingenious suggestion. The body may have been asleep, but not the mind!

Barney's creative power and thorough approach inspired others to do their very best and reach new heights. This was certainly true of much of the work that I did in collaboration with him. One of the exciting things that he, Dave Cochran, and I worked on was solving successfully some of the control and circuit design problems of BART in its early days. Barney's capabilities and accomplishments earned him the greatest respect from everyone who knew him or his work.

Barney was one of my best friends, a favorite colleague, and my boss for many years. He was excellent in all these roles. He never failed to give others credit. He was a truly great man, and I will miss him very much.

Len Cutler
Distinguished Contributor
Technical Staff, HP Laboratories
Palo Alto, California

I have had the privilege of knowing Barney for over 30 years. During this time he spoke with me about physics, chemistry, biology, and especially the correct use of the English language. His deep knowledge of the broad spectrum of natural sciences made me aware, quite early in my association with him, that Barney was probably the only living genius that I have known.

Every so often Barney would visit some of his trusted friends at HP Labs with a few pages of handwritten notes, which I called four-pagers. They usually contained profound conclusions that he derived from his deep understanding of the topics involved. Most of those were Ph.D. thesis material, but some could have competed for the Nobel Prize. He never published those papers, just filed them away, because his interest was already elsewhere by the time he passed them out.

Zvonko Fazarinc
Director, HP Laboratories (retired)
Palo Alto, California

I guess I was a disappointment to Barney when I first came to work for him. He was always correcting someone's English, and as I listened, I soon realized that I was a prime target for his remarks. As soon as I came on the scene, Barney began trying to teach me to speak correctly, and to lose my New York accent. One of his pet peeves was the way I pronounced "saw." He would say, "That's not the way you say it." He kept correcting me and correcting me, and finally I said, "You know, we're not all perfect." He looked at me and shook his head. He still wanted to correct me, but after a while he gave up.

When we were on an eclipse cruise with some astronomers and their friends, the conversation turned to his name. "How did you get the name Bernard?" someone asked. He said, "My mother named me Bernard because she had a great devotion to George Bernard Shaw."

Once I said to him, "Barney, you always seem to be reading and concentrating. Do you ever engage in sports?" He said, "No." I said, "How come?" He said, "It's a waste of time." I asked, "Why is it a waste of time?" He said, "There's too much to learn. There's too much to read. There's too much to do that I don't have time for sports." That was another challenge, because I love sports.

Barney never refused to talk to students, because he loved education so much. My friend Susan Adams teaches at Rancho Milpitas Middle School, and they were working to get a science program started. It's a very diversified school with students from many ethnic groups. Barney was a supporter of that school in his last years, and his interest was a big help. The students have been progressing beautifully. They loved Barney, and he told me that he wanted to go there to meet all the kids, but, of course, he didn't make it. Upon learning that he had died, the faculty and students dedicated a message, "With deepest sympathy to the family of Bernard M. Oliver," and it contained five pages of signatures of all the students. Education has lost a good friend and supporter.

ROSEMARY E. FINNERTY
Assistant to Barney Oliver
HP Laboratories
Palo Alto, California

Barney was "absolutely unique." (I know Barney would insist that "unique" always stands alone; however, in my eyes he *was* absolutely unique!) He was focused, really focused, and demanded clear thought of himself and others. Because he valued thinking time, he often appeared impatient or nearly rude. He did not suffer fools lightly, not because he had a penchant for rudeness, but because he could not stand to see things done poorly or see time, talent, or resources wasted. In many dimensions, he was frugal. His most basic penchant was the quest for new understanding. Because he had pursued new knowledge in so many arenas, he had a sixth sense, a well-developed process that he applied as he, like Gary Cooper, stalked the new domain at high noon—six-shooters on his hips. He had a nose for knowledge wrapped up in a zest for life.

Barney was the greatest of storytellers, who could keep his audience in rapt attention while he worked his way with words, unraveling a tale of St. George and the scientific dragon. Scientists and engineers loved to hear Barney's romantic narratives of how some search for knowledge unfolded.

Barney was a Viking living in the late 20th century. Like his Swedish grandfather who made his way to the gold camps in 1849, Barney was in determined, hot pursuit of the new knowledge frontiers. He never tired of that quest. And we're all the better for it.

DON HAMMOND
Director of HP Laboratories (retired)
Palo Alto, California

Upon joining HP in 1967, I was assigned to the former Avondale (Pennsylvania) Division. We lived for nine years in nearby Wilmington, Delaware, and I became well acquainted with many executives from the neighboring world headquarters of three major chemical companies. Admirable as these fine people were, I couldn't help but observe that we in HP worked in an entirely different atmosphere than they.

One hot summer day in the mid-1970s, I went up to HP's New Jersey Division to attend its annual review. The new building was not quite completed, the air conditioning was not yet fully operational, the outside doors were wide open, and the flies were buzzing around us quite fiercely. I was seated next to Barney Oliver in one row, while immediately in front of us sat Dave Packard. Barney, bless him, was armed with a fly swatter. When one of the little winged miscreants made the fatal mistake of settling momentarily on the back of Dave's head, Barney couldn't resist flattening the intruder with one well-aimed blow.

Understandably startled, Dave rose up, whipped his head around, saw it was Barney, and immediately burst into laugher while the two of them exchanged thumbs-up success signals!

Can you imagine how—and even whether—this revealing little scene would have played out elsewhere in the hallowed halls of most of corporate America?

EMERY ROGERS
HP Manager (retired)
Palo Alto, California

I met Barney when I was only ten or so. My dad was the New England Manufacturer's rep for Hewlett-Packard in the '50s and '60s, during Barney's second career (after Bell Labs). Barney would travel to the East Coast to visit customers and often would have dinner at our home. My early memories were along the lines of: "How could one person know so much about so many subjects?" Back then it ranged from how dolphins communicate, to wine growing in California, and of course—to extraterrestrial life.

My wife and I have two great sons who have grown up with the luck of having met Barney and Dave Packard. Last November, I was telling our older boy—he's twenty-one—that I was going to Barney's service. I briefly related what Barney had done and his passion for SETI. I said, "Barney has this big project that was his passion, he was in search of extraterrestrial intelligence," and my son said, "Gee, Dad, now he *is* one!"

Simple, elegant, Barney would have loved it (even though he might not have believed it!).

Dave Yewell
Formerly with Hewlett-Packard
Now with Notify Corporation

NASA

To: Karen, Gretchen, and Eric—Barney's children:

Please accept my deepest sympathy for your recent loss. Your father will sincerely be missed by all of us at NASA.

Barney Oliver was one of those rare individuals who seized the opportunity to push the envelopes of the known world by his passion, brilliance, and innate curiosity. A visionary engineer, whose individual efforts resulted in the development of the first handheld calculators, Dr. Oliver's accomplishments revolutionized our daily lives in the beginning of an era that has become known for its technological leaps.

In 1971, as co-chair of the Ames Research Center's summer study (*Project Cyclops*), his efforts proved instrumental in defining and establishing the objectives of NASA's first program to search for evidence of advanced extraterrestrial societies. From that introduction, his focus and energy have continued to shape the agency's activities, as exemplified through his recent involvement with NASA's "Roadmap" Planetary Detection Team that has established the strategic plan for the NASA program that will begin to detect and categorize planets throughout the galaxy. He has ensured that the agency would continue on a path that would blend scientific objectives with the cutting edge of technological ability. More important have been his contributions and the impact they have made on the individuals whose lives he touched. The young engineers and scientists he taught, challenged, and inspired will continue to share our future and will become his greatest contribution not only to NASA, but to this nation and the rest of the world.

Please know that your father will never be forgotten.

DANIEL S. GOLDIN
Administrator
National Aeronautics and Space Administration
(Letter dated November 29, 1995)

I was sad to hear of Barney Oliver's passing. He was a very great man.

As you know, I follow the work of the SETI Institute with great care. I believe it is most important, and I am very pleased to see that you are all carrying on.

HANS MARK
Former Director
NASA Ames Research Center
University of Texas at Austin

This is a blow in so many ways. I didn't know Barney very well, but enough so that I can imagine the personal impact on those who did, as well as on the profession. But this is not the end of an era, just part of the beginning—the SETI effort that you all have created will sustain his memory and his intellectual passion.

GEOFF BRIGGS
NASA Ames Research Center, California

We have lost a true friend. What can I say. Like you, my feelings cannot be adequately expressed at this moment. I feel privileged to have known a man of Barney's stature.

His contributions will live on. Heartfelt condolences to his family and to the entire SETI community.

GARY COULTER
Former SETI Program Manager
NASA Headquarters
Washington, D.C.

Barney was welcomed by presidents, kings, and Nobel Prize winners, but he found the time to gently mentor a very junior and unimportant young NASA program manager (me). Since I met him so early in my career (1984), I always expected to find people of Barney's caliber. With few but precious exceptions, no one could hold a candle to him for creativity, invention, kindness, oratory, and a keen sense of fun. I loved the way he rose to every challenge and enjoyed pitting his mind against the absurdities of the government.

LYNN HARPER
Former SETI Program Manager at NASA Headquarters
Now at NASA Ames Research Center, California

I attended Barney's memorial service and was very moved by the expression of love and respect for this giant of a man. It was my honor to know him and try my best to work with him. He was the teacher and I the student. I will be forever grateful for our limited encounter.

ANGELO GUSTAFERRO
Former Director
NASA Ames Research Center
Lockheed Missiles & Space

★ SETI Institute

To live the impossible dream. So few of us have the courage, the natural ability, and above all, the determination to make real the most shining dreams.

We know of one very special person who had this most rare combination of talents. His name was Bernard M. Oliver, but we all know him as Barney Oliver. We gather today to mourn his passing, so untimely on any day, but especially on a day which this year was, for once, improperly called "Thanksgiving." But much more than that, we gather to rejoice in having known such an inspiring human being, and friend to so many, and to rejoice in the many ways he touched us. To some, he was a creative scientific thinker, to others he was primarily a brilliant engineer. To some he was the leader of new scientific or technical projects which tested the limits of human ingenuity and ability. To some he was the father of inventions that have changed the way things are done all over the world, such as the pocket calculator. To some of us here today, he was simply "Father." Finally, to everyone who had the privilege of his company, he was the epitome of intellectual and personal integrity, an example to be mimicked, but almost impossible to equal. It was a privilege to share some of life's greatest moments with him.

I first met Barney in a manner typical of him. We were conducting, as quietly as we could, the first search for extraterrestrial intelligent radio signals, SETI, at the brand-new National Radio Astronomy Observatory in the wilds of West Virginia. In the midst of all the chaos that goes with new experiments, I received a phone call from a "Dr. Oliver," who, though in Washington, intended to come that day to West Virginia to observe our experiment. He was from some little company we had barely heard of— it made some pretty good oscillators, but not much else then. (A few years later, we would marvel at their frequency synthesizers, though.) As it turned out, Barney had thought about SETI for years, and wanted to be part of it. Well, on that day we were given no options. It didn't matter that we were busy. Dr. Oliver was coming. Period. Sure enough, as soon as the clouds cleared, out of the sky came a small plane, which successfully landed on our tiny grass strip in a cow pasture (landings weren't always successful—I had warned him but he didn't care). We called him the "IFO," certainly not a "UFO," and this didn't stand for an "identified flying object." He was the "Incredible Flying Oliver." And so Barney became part of SETI, an enterprise which was to him of the highest interest, priority, and joy for all the rest of his life. I gained a lifelong friend and colleague. SETI is an enterprise whose progress was enhanced greatly by Barney over these last 25 years, and which would be but a pitiful wannabe of a project without his efforts. Eventual success in SETI may well be Barney's most shining monument. We have promised his children that when, finally, the signal is heard, they will be among the first to know.

It is laudable that Barney's accomplishments were recognized. His list of honors boggles the mind: President of the Institute of Electrical and Electronic Engineers; member of *both* the National Academy of Sciences and the National Academy of Engineering, which is almost unheard of; NASA's medal for Exceptional Engineering Achievement; the recipient of the exceptionally rare National Medal of Science in 1986, presented to him by the President of the United States. These are but the tip of the iceberg.

Barney believed that with enough thought, skill, and dedicated people, nothing was beyond our reach. He proved that true time after time. His greatest goal was to reach to the stars, not with a hand, or a blazing rocket, but with waves of radio energy flying at the speed of light. He knew this was the right way. He devoted the last years of his life to SETI, making it progress in any way he could. Thinking through the technical problems. Writing a steady stream of papers. Cajoling people into doing better. Constantly setting his example of intellectual integrity. Finding far more financial support than any of us thought possible. And, recognizing his own mortality, ensuring that the project would go on even though he was gone.

He has given to all of us far more than we have given to him. Now that he can give no more, we honor him. In our own lives, I hope we will follow his example by reaching for our own stars. And, like Barney, doing whatever it takes to achieve the impossible dream.

FRANK DRAKE
Chairman of the Board, SETI Institute
Mountain View, California, and
Professor of Astronomy and Astrophysics
University of California at Santa Cruz

Barney LOVED HP. He loved everything about it. He told me more than once how much he appreciated Dave Packard and Bill Hewlett letting him spend some time on SETI. His technical accomplishments are legend.

George Orwell expected 1984 to be a big year. It certainly was for me. My phone rang one evening that summer. The caller said, "Hello, I'm Barney Oliver. I've been told you know something about research administration. I want to meet with you to discuss SETI." I said OK, we agreed on a time and place, and the phone went dead. I soon learned that this was common for Barney. He had too many things on his mind to bother to say such things as "good-bye." Little did I know that his phone call would be the beginning of the most rewarding professional voyage a person could ever experience. How fortunate I was to work with Barney as we set up the SETI Institute, and to share eleven intense years helping this great man pursue his passion for SETI.

Barney, better than anyone I've ever known, knew exactly when to have fun, when to focus, when to propose a toast. Getting to be part of the fishing gang was an incredible treat for me—I can still hear Barney's voice during the songfest session around the campfire at the close of each day. Even in his last years, Barney had a true devil in him. The SETI folks remember well the warm summer evening a couple of years ago when Barney was zooming around the bumper car track at the Santa Cruz Boardwalk, trying to smash Freeman Dyson while at the same time deftly avoiding the oncoming Frank Drake.

I once asked Barney what one piece of knowledge he would pass on to the next generation if it were his job to do so. His answer: "That every star is a sun." When I look at the night sky, I like to remember Barney and also remember that every star may be someone else's sun.

Tom Pierson
Chief Executive Officer
SETI Institute
Mountain View, California

Knowing Barney since 1975 has forever changed my life. Though I was terrified of him when I first met him, through the years he became one of the best, most loyal and understanding friends I have ever had. He, Charles Seeger, and I had weekly lunches together after our SETI staff meetings, and over the years we shared laughter and tears, frustrations and joys—and in the process, we all grew stronger. Because Barney's credo was that he was *nothing* if he was not honest, I (and all of us) always knew where he (and we) stood. He never waivered.

Barney's kindness would show through as his eyes grew teary when he'd tell the story of how Hewlett and Packard helped Charlie Litton years ago by allowing his workers to use HP lab facilities at night after Litton's place had burned out. He liked knowing he worked for men who cared. He cared, as well.

A longtime colleague of Barney's told me that we might rue the day that we met Barney, because we would never again have in our lives a person of such wisdom, wit, vision, directness, humor, and genuine kindness. Many beings inhabit this planet, but only a small percentage leave such an impact on so many lives. Barney was a true trailblazer.

I know his children have lost a *big light* in their lives (we all have). Thanks to Barney, twenty years later I stand taller and more confident because of him, but my soul will always miss him.

VERA BUESCHER
Special Projects Coordinator
SETI Institute
Mountain View, California

I first met Barney through his writing in *Project Cyclops*. This document proved that we could communicate with other technologies like ours over thousands of light-years of interstellar space. To me, this was a stunning realization, a fact which I had never known but which was undeniably true. The report was so excitingly written, with such eloquence and vision, that my wife Carol, who was reading it to me, became as fascinated as I. She read the entire document aloud, not even stopping for sleep until it was complete, down to every appendix and equation. Then Carol and I talked about all the incredible ideas and concepts developed in that lovingly crafted piece of writing. We fell asleep hoping someday to meet the man who told that tale. Years later, we did meet Barney, and I was privileged to work with him on SETI during the last 20 years of his life. He was my friend and teacher. He was that rare kind of dreamer who could make his dreams real. Even more remarkably, he could teach other people the same skill.

A few years ago Carol died suddenly, and Barney came to my office. I had given the eulogy at Carol's memorial, and Barney read me the one he had written for his mother. We talked about Life, the Universe, and Death. His words comforted me because our approach to life had so many common elements. He helped me through a difficult time. He was a true friend.

Though Barney was not noted for his patience, he was patient with me. I am a physicist, totally blind since birth. Blindness changes the way one analyzes physical and mathematical problems. In particular, communicating ideas to the outside world and getting information from that world is difficult because using paper and pencil is impossible. This must be compensated by careful verbal description or computer-assisted interactions. Such difficulties forced development of unusual intuitive ways to find solutions to problems. The methods Barney helped me develop to find weak signals from the stars were the result of this process. He always had the time to explain things to me and let me explain my insights to him. Even more important, he subjected my ideas to the same ruthless criticism he applied to work generally. He gave me no special treatment. At times this was painful, but because of our years spent in the relentless search for truth, I grew to love Barney. I loved him not because he was easy to live with, but because he made me grow. I am a smarter and better person today than I would have been without Barney. For that I shall always be grateful.

I will think often of Barney. He taught me to be fearless and honest in pursuing truth. He showed me how to investigate something seriously, not just casually. He showed many how to play the great game of science and engineering that finds new knowledge. His friends will continue to play that game, in the incredible, serious way that Barney taught us to play. And so, undoubtedly, Barney Oliver and his ideas will continue to change the world.

KENT CULLERS
SETI Institute
Mountain View, California

There has been a great sadness in my heart since Barney's death. Mostly, it is a deep sense of loss for all of the people who worked with and loved Barney. It is also a sense of missed opportunity, as I had only recently begun to know Barney, and to enjoy his unique and special qualities. Years ago, I read about a conversation with Ernest Hemingway. He was asked how he developed such a clear and concise writing style—and how he managed to capture the human spirit at its most basic level. Hemingway responded, "I have a built-in, shockproof crap detector." Barney always reminded me of that story. For me, Barney was a man who thought, spoke, and led clearly. He asked the central questions at the right times, and, without hesitation, pointed toward the correct path. I suspect that his directness was intimidating to some, but for me, it was wonderful. Too often we get caught in a haze of words and lose direction. I will miss his leadership, his humor, and his direct view of life.

EDNA DEVORE
Educational Program Office
SETI Institute
Mountain View, California

Barney was loved by all of us more than he, or even we knew, until now. One looks back on such a life of service to mankind (how many millions have been saved from a lifetime of calculations by Barney's efforts to produce the first handheld calculator, for example?). One feels humble to have known such a person with an unspoken, yet ever-present, unselfish reason for being. Barney worked at the limits of what humans thought was possible, ever pushing those limits farther. His wonderfully abrupt exposure of falsehood and his unyielding integrity when it came to scientific truth were refreshing to all who knew him and did their homework (and terrifying to those who didn't). One could rely on Barney to bring out the best in one's work well done (and always discover some new facet of it). One could also rely on Barney for a well-earned rebuke for not thinking. He thus set a high standard that showed his great respect for truth as well as for his junior colleagues who sometimes got such rebukes. They were always greatly appreciated. But a slight smile and a sparkle in the eye from Barney when a new idea was presented was the best reward.

To present something intellectually new to Barney was a rare event, and to have the idea respected by him was to feel on solid intellectual footing. I am honored to have known Barney Oliver, and am privileged to have had his example to aspire to. His life example is still present for us to emulate, and for that I will always be very grateful.

Laurance Doyle
SETI Institute
Mountain View, California

I had the honor of working with Barney from 1989 to 1995. He was one of the first people I met when I came on board the SETI ship, and from the very beginning I think we had a special connection. He could be intimidating (if you allowed it), but also funny and charming. More than once he would sit at the computer with me, trying to help me figure out T_eX, which was the software we used for his technical papers. Once I got the hang of it, it was great fun to be able to produce a beautiful rendition of his brilliant thoughts.

To know someone so special and so downright awesome is a gift. I thank my lucky stars for the gift of knowing Barney.

Chris Neller
SETI Institute
Mountain View, California

I wish I had known Barney better than I did, but I value the memories I have. He will always be a part of each person he touched in some way or another. The first week I was here, we had the regular monthly SETI staff meeting hosted by John Billingham. I remember walking into the meeting room, filled with 20 or more people, feeling a little nervous and uncomfortable. Though my first week's experience of meeting people on the SETI team was great, I was still a bit nervous about going to this first meeting.

No one I had met during the first week had arrived at the meeting yet, so I found my way to an empty seat at the back of the room. After being seated, I looked around again to see if anyone I knew was there. Not recognizing anyone immediately, I began to wonder if I had gone to the right meeting room. I then noticed this man getting up from his chair across the room. He made his way through the crowd of people and came over to where I was seated. He came up, shook my hand and said, "My name is Barney Oliver. I noticed a new face in the room, so I thought I would come over and introduce myself. What part of the project are you working on?"

I proceeded to tell him who I was and that I worked in the signal detection group for Kent Cullers. We spoke for a few minutes and then he welcomed me to the team and to the meeting, and he returned to his seat. I remember feeling very much at ease after this conversation. It wasn't until later in the meeting that I realized who Barney was.

To some, this may seem insignificant, but for some reason this memory remains with me. Maybe it is because each time I interacted with Barney after the first meeting, he always greeted me with the same kindness. Though many will remember Barney as the one who took on the world with his great technical abilities, when I think of Barney, I will remember the wonderfully kind gentleman who took the time to make welcome a newcomer to the SETI team.

ALAN PATRICK
Signal Detection Team
SETI Institute
Mountain View, California

When Barney joined HP it was a chance to work with friends he respected and to return to where he had been born and raised. As HP grew, he quietly shared his financial good fortune with causes and people he respected who needed help. Here are two examples.

He admired the gumption of the Monterey Institute for Research in Astronomy, which had set out to build an optical observatory (near Monterey) of a size sufficient for serious research. It included facilities for members of the general public in the Monterey area to view the heavens away from blinding city lights and to acquire a deeper understanding of what astronomers were after. All this without seeking any form of governmental funding.

The telescope was nearing completion and, now, a building to house it was required. More fund-raising. At this point Barney stepped in, promising to match dollar-for-dollar up to two hundred thousand dollars of other funds they managed to raise. Result? The Oliver Observatory.

Early one summer, Larry joined our SETI project at NASA Ames Research Center in Mountain View, California. He had yet to finish high school in San Jose, but he had a temperament and skills that fitted in well with our most unusual group. He came back each summer even when he went on to Caltech as a scholarship student.

Remember the violent inflation of the late '70s and early '80s? One day, Larry came in to tell us that Caltech had canceled his scholarship because the house where his parents and younger siblings lived had increased in value beyond a limit permitting his scholarship. Larry's family had even less money than before because they had to look forward to higher taxes. While some of us thought of how we would like to torture the MBAs who invented that gimmick, Barney reached for his checkbook and wrote a check that gave Larry all he needed to complete his studies at Caltech.

Yes, Barney could be gruff. And particularly so in his later years when pain haunted every waking hour. But he was a gentle pussycat to those with well-grounded ids and egos. We teased him once upon a time with the title "Gruff Old Silicon Valley Warlord" and photographed him against a background dominated by a huge highway advertisement for "Barney's Used Cars."

Hang it all, we will miss him; he was a rare wonder.

CHARLES SEEGER
SETI Astronomer (retired)
NASA Ames Research Center and
SETI Institute
Mountain View, California

Thinking about moments with Barney is like fingering nuggets plucked from a prospector's pan. Multifaceted and obviously valuable, such memories are accorded the best shelf space in my mind.

I recall occasionally sharing a dinner table with Barney, an experience that was simultaneously unnerving and enlightening. Any opinion, disguised as statement, was subject to challenge. "Why do you say that?" Barney would bellow. Why indeed? His skepticism and unrelenting lust for truth often forced me to either back off my glib remark or quickly try to arrange my mental ducks. The latter was always good exercise.

While his wit was steel-edged, Barney himself was like nougat candy; he had a soft center. One desultory afternoon, Barney was reminiscing to me about his time at Bell Labs. "We were working on television—it was clearly the next thing," he said. "But then the war came along, and we all got involved with radar . . ." He looked to the side and paused. "You know," he continued softly, "it's enough to make you cry. The country was united then, in a way it hasn't been since." Barney was silent. His eyes visibly misted over. And so did mine.

SETH SHOSTAK
Public Programs Scientist
SETI Institute
Mountain View, California

This morning when I awoke here in the mountains, I knew that the Earth had become smaller because it was no longer required to support the weight of the giant we knew as Barney Oliver.

On paper, Barney wondered whether the physics that controlled the ravening chaos of the cosmos and produced the delicate cherry blossom, and even we curious humans did, in fact, operate elsewhere. On paper, he wondered whether the universe is indeed destined for life. In his heart he knew the answer. Yet his enormous intellect demanded proof. My profound regret is that we have not yet been able to provide that evidence for him. All of us are fortunate that Barney followed his heart, and I miss him. Someday we shall find the proof; perhaps he will smile.

JILL TARTER
Director, Project Phoenix
SETI Institute
Mountain View, California

⭐ Colleagues in the United States

Condolences to the family . . . my greatest respect for his ingenuity and energy, particularly in the World War II years.

BRITTON CHANCE
University of Pennsylvania
Philadelphia, Pennsylvania

Silent Key—Barney Oliver: (The phrase "silent key" is used by radio amateurs to refer to the quiet telegraph key of one who has passed.)

Barney had a keen intellect and a very dominant personality. I remember fondly many pleasant nights spent at Barney's home in the hills overlooking Palo Alto: nights spent discussing many philosophical and technical items—usually with a pitcher of gin and tonic on the table. It was at Barney's home that I first heard CD music—he had just returned from Japan with a Sony prototype, at a time when there were only 10 in the world. He played it through his (in)famous "BMO" amplifier (packaged in HP instrument cabinets) through his own design bass reflex speaker system that used his fireplace as an acoustic chamber. As a young, impressionable, budding technocrat, I was duly impressed.

It was during one of those late-night sessions that I told Barney about AMSAT (an organization of amateurs who build and send communication satellites into orbit for the use of radio amateurs). He was taken by the fact that we were actually building technically sophisticated hardware in our basements. Barney invited me to spend the next day (a Saturday as I recall) at HP Labs on Page Mill Road, and gave me free rein of their instrument storeroom for AMSAT. He also arranged for HP to donate some really nifty test equipment to AMSAT, some of which is still in use at AMSAT's Orlando lab facility.

Barney never was an amateur operator, but he was our friend. For those of us who had the pleasure to meet and work with him, he made a profound impact on our lives. He was a friend and supporter of AMSAT. He will be missed!

TOM CLARK
Astronomer
AMSAT and NASA Goddard Space Flight Center
Greenbelt, Maryland

On Thanksgiving Day, 1995, Dr. Bernard "Barney" Oliver passed away, after a dozen years of fighting a chronic heart condition and other illnesses. In one moment, we lost the strongest SETI advocate and one of the best engineers of the century. We also lost a person unique in his ability to foster new ideas and the people to carry them through.

Long before Barney was a SETI expert, he was a damn good engineer. With the strength of strong physics and engineering educations at Stanford and Caltech, Barney spent a dozen years at Bell Labs before joining his friends Bill Hewlett and David Packard at their young company. Barney was a key player in making HP the giant it is today. His work in the calculator arena took an expensive lab instrument and made it a must-have device. In other words, Barney helped kill the slide rule. Think about that the next time you add up your expenses or plot some complex curve. As one of the fathers of the calculator, Barney could claim to be stepfather of the personal computer.

There is some irony in this: Barney had a healthy disregard for computers. He honestly saw people succumbing to *computeritis*. One engineer told me how Barney welcomed his HP colleagues at a staff party by saying: "Sorry we don't see each other more often, but you all seem to be glued to those TV screens." Of course the engineers weren't watching *Laverne and Shirley* but were blasting away on their PCs with their monitors. Barney's good-natured quip was a reminder that the best computer is on our shoulders.

In the past few years I saw Barney only a handful of times. On one occasion I recall having the privilege of joining him at his banquet table. We discussed SETI, inventing, being an entrepreneur. Fighting off the effects of medication and pain, Barney relished the memories of a recent fishing trip, letting me see a piece of the private joy that kept him going. Afterwards I felt that there was so much more for me to learn, and so much more of life to experience. And now Barney is gone, leaving me and others with a profound sense that there remains much to be completed. And so along with Barney's colleagues and friends I say: "Goodbye old friend, gone never to be forgotten." It is time for us, and SETI, to carry on.

NATHAN COHEN
Boston University

It's very sad to hear of Barney Oliver's passing. He was a true pioneer in so many ways. I will treasure more the moments that I have shared with him over the years.

LEONARD DAVID
Space Data Resources
Washington, D.C.

I just heard that Barney died. I'm sorry. Barney was at a two-day meeting early this year; we hadn't had a chance to talk so much since the Estonia conference in 1981. He was sharp and full of ideas. He always challenged us to do our best, to enjoy life to the fullest. I will miss that deep booming voice and the twinkle in his eye.

SETI, no, Intelligence, has lost its best friend. He was the glue that held us all to our mission. Who will pick up the scepter and lead us now?

GEORGE GATEWOOD
Allegheny Observatory
Pittsburgh, Pennsylvania

News of the death of Barney Oliver comes as a shock and with great sadness. As an instructor of bioastronomy for over 20 years, I have followed his career and accomplishments from afar with great respect and awe.

R. DWAYNE HIGHFILL
Professor of Astronomy
Rio Hondo College
Whittier, California

Barney Oliver had a profound influence on the development of electronics at HP and at Stanford, particularly as Stanford and the electronics industry here were becoming nationally visible. I want to recall a few instances of his contributions and interactions with the Stanford community.

I came to Stanford from the Bell Telephone Laboratories three years after Barney came from Bell Labs in 1952, to join William Hewlett and David Packard, with whom he had attended classes at Stanford. Particularly during the years when I was chairman of electrical engineering at Stanford, from 1964 to 1980, Barney Oliver, in my perception, had the most impact on graduate study in electrical engineering at Stanford of any of our industry colleagues. He gave many seminars in fields of his interest and accomplishment. His questions and comments at any meeting added interest.

Personal contact with Barney made it clear that he enjoyed work in science and engineering. He had very high standards for himself and for his colleagues. A mutual friend of Barney's and mine at Bell Labs came out annually to recruit outstanding Ph.D. candidates for Bell. In the '60s he came to see me after having spent the morning with Barney. He said to me, "Barney is the smartest man I know. He should have his Nobel Prize by now. But he spent the whole morning talking to me about some ideas for an electronic desktop calculator." Those "ideas" were central in producing the handheld scientific and business calculators in which HP still holds a dominant position.

For many years Barney was on Stanford's School of Engineering Advisory Council; he was chairman of that council during the late '70s when three colleagues and I proposed establishing the Center for Integrated Systems. At the request of Dean Kays we presented our plans to the Advisory Council. Barney had tough questions to ask, after which he became a strong supporter and advocate for the Center. In many other proposals in the School of Engineering, his interaction was crucial and his advocacy, which had to be earned, was persuasive.

Barney was a remarkable man and a good friend. He will be sorely missed, but his personal and technical contributions to this community and to the world will have a lasting, important impact.

JOHN G. LINVILL
Canon USA Professor of Engineering, Emeritus
Stanford University

To: Karen, Gretchen, and Eric Oliver:

On behalf of the University of California, Santa Cruz, let me express my condolences upon the passing of your father, Barney Oliver. He was a creative giant who emerged from the Santa Cruz area long before the University was located here. We were delighted that in his later years he chose to become engaged with the campus through our Natural Sciences Dean's Council and the creation of the Priscilla Newton Oliver Endowed Scholarship in Theater Arts. He gave wise counsel to our Deans of Natural Science from 1986 up to his passing. We are also both honored by and indebted to his decision to permanently endow a scholarship in your mother's memory here at UC Santa Cruz.

We are all saddened by your father's passing. He will be missed. I do hope that as you occasionally return to the area of his roots you will feel free to come and visit the Santa Cruz campus. We are truly honored that the Oliver name is permanently linked with us.

KARL S. PISTER
Chancellor
University of California at Santa Cruz

The death of Barney Oliver recalls the glory days of American science and engineering. Those were the days when Bell Laboratories and David Sarnoff Research Laboratories squared off against each other in a much-observed research rivalry, when American research engineering was at its best, unencumbered by the "need" for commercial practicality.

Some of us own *Electronic Measurements and Instrumentation,* the classic 1971 McGraw-Hill text edited by Oliver and John Cage. Oliver wrote the first three chapters of that text. Look for a copy if you want to evaluate an oscilloscope or understand why peak-to-peak detection is better than simple peak detection, or learn how to measure a signal in the presence of noise. Oliver wrote:

> *New discoveries in science provided new instruments for the study of nature and these studies produced new discoveries in a regenerative buildup that has been accelerating for the last two centuries and continues to accelerate today. . . . Where science will take us in the future, no one knows. That is what makes it such an exciting adventure. . . . The*

role of science is to discover the laws of nature and how they operate in complex systems. The role of engineering is to apply the discoveries of science to human needs. Scientists make discoveries that increase our understanding of the world. Engineers make inventions intended to increase our productivity (and thereby our standard of living), our mobility, and (it is hoped) our ability to survive.

I will miss Bernard Oliver. He made my life better. Who, I wonder, will do the same for my children?

STAN RUNYON
TEST POINTS
Electronic Engineering Times, *December 11, 1995*

Barney was truly a pioneer in SETI, someone willing to venture into a barely known region of science to advance our understanding and technical progress. I first met Barney in the 1970s at a meeting at the University of California at Santa Cruz on planetary detection. He came and discussed *Project Cyclops.* His dedication to furthering the science of SETI over the many years when there has been so much controversy is a tribute to him. *Project Phoenix,* I see, as Barney's legacy, something I hope will outlive him in time but keep him alive in spirit.

DAVID SODERBLOM
Space Telescope Science Institute
Baltimore, Maryland

⬛ SETI Around the World

Puerto Rico

Our paths did not cross very often, but whenever they did I was struck by Barney's enthusiasm and his mature and sound judgment. Our meetings were nearly always in connection with SETI and the involvement of Arecibo in that project. I came to appreciate Barney's support for Arecibo and the upgrading project. I suspect that his intervention and pulling of strings behind the scenes had a lot to do with the SETI support we obtained, which was a necessity to get our plans realized. We have lost a true friend in Barney.

TOM HAGFORS
Director
Arecibo Telescope
Arecibo, Puerto Rico

I have shared with many here at Arecibo Observatory the benefits of Barney Oliver's long association with the Cornell community, and the Arecibo Observatory in particular. I first met him during his visit to Puerto Rico as a member of the Arecibo Advisory Board in the mid-'70s. Barney's hallmark enthusiasm and penetrating questions immediately set him apart. Over the years he has been a strong advocate of the Observatory, for SETI and all areas of research. He played an important role in providing support for the Gregorian upgrading of the Arecibo telescope, and we are sincerely sorry that he will not be here to see this completed.

Let me say on behalf of my wife Jean and myself, and the entire National Astronomy and Ionosphere Center community, that we shall all sorely miss him.

MIKE DAVIS
Arecibo Observatory
Arecibo, Puerto Rico

United States

Barney is responsible for steering my life into the field of SETI. I was fortunate to have been chosen by him as one of the participants in *Project Cyclops*. That summer was very exciting intellectually and prompted me to return to Ohio State and start what became the first full-time SETI program.

Barney's disagreement with some of my ideas over the years always goaded me to even more effort and deeper investigations to convince him otherwise. This caused me to learn more about many things that I would not otherwise have studied, and I benefited from that greatly. Some of my greatest accomplishments have been in moving Barney from the "No" position to the "Maybe" position!

ROBERT DIXON
SETI Observer
Ohio State University Radio Observatory
Columbus, Ohio

On behalf of all of us here at The Planetary Society, and particularly for Carl (Sagan), Bruce (Murray), and myself, please accept our condolences for the loss of our good friend and colleague, Barney Oliver. Barney's intellectual leadership in our common interest in the search for extraterrestrial intelligence was matched only by his able, determined, and energetic leadership of the NASA program.

It's been a tough couple of years for our colleagues in the former NASA SETI program. We deeply admire how they have kept their vision and increased their efforts, despite those setbacks. We trust that Barney's death will not diminish the vision nor hamper the efforts. Please convey our condolences to his family and other close friends.

LOUIS FRIEDMAN
Executive Director
The Planetary Society
Pasadena, California

I remember vividly my first audience with Barney Oliver. Not the printed name on the ingenious *Project Cyclops* report, but the real thing: Barney was a Force of Nature, a power to be reckoned with. When he spoke, it was with clarity and authority: "Not now, not ever" was his pronouncement on Earth's chances for interstellar travel.

Here was the quintessential industrial scientist, creator of an authoritative primer on *Thermal and Quantum Noise* (Barney the intellectual), designer of an ingenious isochronous conical pendulum clock (Barney the inventor), author of delightful short pieces on "Heron's Remarkable Triangle Area Formula" or "Power Series with Fibonacci Coefficients" (Barney the historian), creator of *Project Cyclops,* the primer on the Search for Extraterrestrial Intelligence (Barney the missionary), publisher of tracts on "Galactic Colonization and Other Flights of Fancy" (Barney the gadfly)—all beautiful, in conception, in execution, and especially in expression—and just the tip of the iceberg, I imagine, because Barney was, throughout, directing research at the most successful scientific instrument corporation that the world has seen.

Barney Oliver was a giant, even among the likes of Frank Drake, Phil Morrison, and Carl Sagan. Scientist, technologist, visionary extraordinaire. We will all miss him terribly.

PAUL HOROWITZ
Professor of Physics
Harvard University

Just a few moments ago I read that Barney Oliver had passed away. Please convey my condolences to his family. I was looking forward to "going into battle" again with Barney at the next Optical SETI Conference. Sadly, that is not to be. Even though we differed very strongly in our opinions as to the relative merits of the microwave and optical approaches to SETI, I much respected his contributions to American science and technology.

He will be sorely missed by this nation, and those in the worldwide SETI community. I will miss him too.

STUART A. KINGSLEY
ETI Photonics
Director, The Columbus Optical SETI Observatory
Columbus, Ohio

The Barney Oliver anecdotes are legion. An EE Ph.D. degree from Caltech in hand, he had established himself as one of Bell Labs' most creative microwave receiver designers before I was even born. Frank Drake loves to tell how Barney dropped out of the sky in a single-engine Mooney to visit Drake at Green Bank, West Virginia, in 1960, as Drake was preparing to launch *Project Ozma*, the very first SETI effort. As vice president of R&D at Hewlett-Packard, Barney spearheaded the development of the scientific pocket calculator.

I've always felt you can tell a great deal about a person by how he or she chooses to unwind. After hearing Barney give a talk on Cyclops at Lockheed/Sunnyvale in mid-1997, several of us went to Charley Brown's Steak House for dessert. The group included Barney, Nick Marshall (a longtime SETI enthusiast, who invited me to Barney's talk), my then-wife Suk, and me. Nick, though Hungarian, had been educated in Paris, and ordered something sweet and gooey from the French pastry cart. Suk, who was pregnant with our son Andrew, ordered ice cream, and joked about pickles on the side. My ethnic roots drove me to order New York style cheesecake. And then Barney blew us all away by ordering a double Scotch on the rocks. Suddenly I felt I understood something of the source of his genius. I told him so; Barney tried to deadpan, then grinned that warm engaging smile of his, and sipped his Scotch.

What words can one use as a fitting tribute to a man who taught us how to dream. It will be difficult ever dreaming at so grand a scale without Barney.

H. Paul Shuch
Executive Director
The SETI League, Inc.
Little Ferry, New Jersey

Barney was an esteemed colleague and leader in the SETI enterprise. We benefited from his wisdom in all our discussions, and I was continually amazed at the breadth of his vision. As recently as at our retreat in Berkeley only days before he died, we heard new ideas from him and enjoyed his valuable criticism in all our discussions. He was a valued and generous friend, and we will miss him.

Jack Welch
Former Director, Radio Astronomy Lab
University of California at Berkeley

I am saddened to hear about Barney's death. Barney had a profound influence on my life. In 1971 (I was in high school) I heard him give a great talk on SETI, so I read his *Project Cyclops* report—and I've been hooked on this stuff ever since.

When I had dinner with Barney at the SETI retreat last week, I was pleased to observe that he was still a powerful thinker, with clever insights, and as stubborn and argumentative as ever.

DAN WERTHIMER
Project SERENDIP
University of California at Berkeley

Australia

We were all upset to hear of Barney's death. Please pass on our deepest sympathy to his family from all of us at the Australia Telescope National Facility, especially from our *Project Phoenix* team.

Those of us fortunate enough to meet Barney will remember him fondly.

JOHN BROOKS
Acting Director
Australia Telescope National Facility

I was deeply shocked to hear about the death of Barney Oliver, and have been asked by both the Dean of the Faculty of Business and Technology, Professor Roger Alexander, and the Director of the Office of Development and External Relations, Paul McShane, to extend our sympathies on behalf of UWS Macarthur to both Barney's family and everyone at the SETI Institute.

Although I had only one brief conversation with Barney, I am well aware of the special person he was and his unfailing support for the Institute. It is a loss I know will be felt by all of you.

Bobbie Vaile, whom I know has already written to you, says it is a time to share the good memories of Barney rather than be sad. A difficult task, but I have long learned not to question Bobbie's wisdom in these matters.

CAROL OLIVER
University of Western Sydney, Macarthur
Sydney, Australia

I only met Barney briefly over the last three years, and yet it was clear that Barney Oliver was a man of great accomplishment and a keen searching mind. Such a man was also striving for the best despite the challenges in his tasks, and his singular dedication to the advancement of the SETI Institute goals and directives was striking.

It is the drive of men such as Barney that inspires and encourages others to strive themselves, and that is essential for good teamwork. None of it is easy for anyone, and the leadership he provided is critically important.

I, along with all of you, will miss Barney.

BOBBIE VAILE
University of Western Sydney, Macarthur
Sydney, Australia

It really is very saddening to hear of Barney Oliver's passing. His efforts over the years made a big impression on me. I can remember back in the early '70s when I first came across his *Project Cyclops* report. And there were so many more things that I would have loved to discuss with him. His sharp mind was almost scary, the way it could pick out the weak links in any grand vision. But I feel blessed for having known him, however fleetingly. I'll miss him, as I'm sure will all of the SETI Institute.

KELVIN WELLINGTON
Australia Telescope Facility
Epping, Australia

Canada

Barney, Charlie Seeger, John Billingham, Vera Buescher, and all the people at SETI have been dear to my heart all through my professional life. SETI introduced me to brain evolution, Barney introduced me to Louis Alvarez, and my SETI friends sustained me in the dinosauroid saga and even published my papers! Do you know that Barney was my roommate at the Santa Cruz conference? He was so decent to me, in spite of my being so obviously not his peer.

Since 1981 my little HP11C has been with me everywhere I have gone, from the Junggar Gobi to the Western Desert of Egypt—even my wife has not been with me as much.

If a man may say so without behaving shamefully, I love you all and honor the memory of Barney.

DALE RUSSELL
National Museum of Natural Science
Ottawa, Canada

Russia

It was a deep sorrow that we learned of the death of Dr. Bernard M. Oliver.

On behalf of the Russian SETI community, please accept our condolences over the loss of a man whose work and personality have contributed so much to world science and technology. His devotion to his work won him the regard and admiration of all who knew him.

Please convey our deep sympathy to his family.

NIKOLAY S. KARDASHEV
Sergey F. Likhachev Astro Space Center
Moscow, Russia

I knew Barney through occasional SETI meetings. But every such meeting was illuminated and warmed by Barney's unparalleled goodness, simplicity, and cleverness. He was a rare type of human being—with whom you feel easy and cozy from the very first contact and never have a chance to be disenchanted.

VLADIMIR STRELNITSKI
Russian SETI Scientist
Now at National Air & Space Museum
Washington, D.C.

⭐ Personal Friends and Associates

Dear Tom: My condolences, in particular, to you. While Barney's loss is great to his family, to SocialTech, and to SETI, I suspect one of the greatest losses is to you personally.

BOB ASQUITH
President
SocialTech
Burlingame, California

Barney was a brilliant man and a man of strong convictions. In fact, I felt intimidated in his presence because of his towering intellect.

With all his brilliance, he was a compassionate and concerned citizen, truly dedicated to bettering the condition of all humankind. I count it a privilege to be among his friends.

REED LARSON
President
National Right to Work Committee
Springfield, Virginia

I first met Barney Oliver when he arrived at Highlanders Camp in the Bohemian Grove, as a guest of Bill Hewlett, in the summer of 1985. Barney had just joined the Bohemian Club.

Barney loved to sit in front of the outdoor fire at night and discuss anything and everything. He always had a strong opinion on almost every subject, and he was uniquely knowledgeable about most all of the discussion items.

Barney loved the frequent evening sing-alongs by the fire with top-notch musicians and singers coming to visit Highlanders, having a wee Scotch, and sharing their expertise with us. Barney knew the words to almost every song ever written. He had a fine group singing voice that helped make the Highlanders' participation palatable.

Barney added a very special ingredient to the aura of Highlanders Camp that will never be duplicated— a one of a kind, gem of a human being who comes along only once in a great while. We all have been supremely fortunate to have been good friends of this very special person.

DICK MADIGAN
Fellow Highlander
Atherton, California

Of all the fine people I've met throughout the one and one-half years of this SocialTech project, Barney impressed me by far the most. Of course, considering his achievements, that's hardly surprising. He was really the one who made it possible for SocialTech to become a reality instead of just a good idea.

I was really looking forward to continuing to meet with and know Barney (a co-founder and charter board member of SocialTech) during the course of our development and growth.

MICK RUTHVEN
SocialTech
Burlingame, California

It was my privilege to attend Barney's memorial service and hear the nice things that were said about him. We had the greatest admiration for Dr. Oliver because of his intellect, but also because he was such a nice person. He certainly will be missed.

FRED AND NELDA WARREN
Construction contractor who did repairs for Barney on his property
Mountain View, California

To the Family of Barney Oliver:

I knew Barney as a member of the Highlanders Camp at the Bohemian Club. He was one of the most interesting men I have ever met, and I always looked forward to seeing him at Camp events. I enjoyed hours of debate on a wide variety of subjects; his knowledge was incredible and rarely did I ever find myself the winner of any contest of correct information.

As I know all of you will, I too shall miss him, and will think of him every time I visit the Highlanders Camp.

ERIC P. WENTE
Fellow Highlander
Livermore, California

In 1969 Barney Oliver telephoned attorney Harry Lucas, his old friend from Santa Cruz High School, for help with a legal problem. I was the new law associate. Mr. Lucas instructed me to telephone Barney about an agricultural lease. Barney's voice was so loud that I held the receiver away from my ear. He instructed me to go to the family homestead, Rancho Soquel, and survey 19 acres of farmland that Barney had leased as a Christmas tree farm. I inspected the premises the next day. The tenant had departed, removed all the trees, and left 19 acres of evenly spaced holes of a routine depth and diameter. The following day, I made what I thought was a thorough report to Barney. Not quite. Barney asked what the number of holes was. He wanted the exact number or a very close estimate of the holes so that he could calculate the amount of topsoil the farmer had taken with him. That was my first lesson from Barney. Get your facts! Many learning experiences followed over the next quarter century.

In early 1994, California Governor Pete Wilson appointed me Judge of the Superior Court. Once appointed, I was required to advise Barney that I could no longer act as his attorney. Barney would not accept that fact, and said that since I could no longer be his attorney, he was appointing me his property manager in Santa Cruz.

The last long conversation I had with Barney was at Rancho Soquel on the patio under the trees a few months before he passed away. It was a cool, sunny, summer afternoon. He reminisced that as a small boy he used to lie on a blanket at night in the yard with his mother, Margaret More Oliver. Together they identified the constellations and other celestial bodies. That was a warm memory for him. Both Margaret and Barney's father, William, were 1906 graduates of the University of California, Berkeley. Margaret became a legend as a Santa Cruz County schoolteacher. William was an engineer and he eventually became the County Engineer. In the barn, father and son repaired machinery, invented easier ways to use farm tools, tinkered with new gadgets, and worked on the household radio.

Recently I found a handwritten letter from eight-year-old Barney. He was visiting relatives in San Luis Obispo. He wrote to his parents, "Uncle Perry says he has a telescope and maybe he will let us look through it. He says he can see two of Jupiter's moons." The seed was planted early.

Barney's rich ideas and spirit of discovery will be with us always.

ROBERT B. YONTS, JR.
Judge of the Superior Court
Santa Cruz, California

★ Family

Excerpts from the memorial tribute by Barney's son, Eric:

Most of you knew my father as a professional or a colleague in the scientific or engineering field. I knew him as Dad. As a child we did very few childish activities together, but Dad saw to it that I had plenty of wonderful toys for Christmas. Mom and I practically lived in Norney's. As I grew up, Dad and I spent many weekends working on various projects at Hewlett-Packard's wonderful woodshop at the old HP building. We would go to Kirk's for lunch and a beer. I'm sure I drank my first beer before anybody at school did.

When I was in high school, Dad taught me geometry—it was rough for me at first, but soon I was witness to Dad's great insight as a problem solver. Dad used the axioms and postulates like most people use a vice, screwdriver, and pliers. He could see through most problems because he loved to play with mathematics as if it were a great game. Later, when I encountered second-degree differential equations, he invited me to his office on Sunday afternoons, where we would spend joyous hours solving harmonic problems. Once, at the end of a long problem, Dad repeated the solution in the complex number plane. I remember because I was speechless on the way home.

I worked as a technician at Shugart's R&D hard drive laboratory in the late 1970s. At Shugart, I knew a mechanical engineer from Terrale named Max, and one day he invited me to his office. He asked me point blank if I knew about the things my Dad had done in the '40s, '50s, and '60s. "Not really," I responded, so Max told me about radar, pulse code modulation, and Dad's work at HP. When I later confronted Dad, I asked why he had not told me about these accomplishments. He said he didn't want to intimidate me. But I was happy for what Max told me—I was so very proud of Dad.

Dad's insightful vision brought forth the scientific calculator and later, the search for intelligent life in the universe. He was by no means alone in these endeavors, but he had a lot of passion to see them through. When Luis Alvarez came up with his theory of the extinction of the dinosaurs by means of a gigantic meteor, I remember how this impressed Dad, for he loved elegant solutions to complex problems.

When Dad got time off from Hewlett-Packard to do the initial *Project Cyclops* report, I'll never forget the nonstop work he put in on it. He would come home for dinner and no sooner after taking a sip of his martini, he would be writing.

I once asked Dad about the impact of contact with another intelligence—he sort of smiled and said, "Perhaps if the whole worked knew we were being observed from afar, we would be less likely to commit suicide in a nuclear war."

I am convinced that someday a group of wealthy entrepreneurs will get together and fund SETI adequately. When they do, they will own the most astounding e-mail system ever conceived.

WILLIAM ERIC OLIVER
San Francisco, California

Excerpts from the memorial tribute by Barney's daughter, Gretchen:

I wish to thank all of you for coming today, and I would like to extend special thanks to all of you who have contributed to the beautiful celebration of our father's life. Although all of you are here because you knew my dad, I am one of only three people in the world to be able to share some thoughts on the unique and difficult experience of being my father's child.

There may be some who will accuse me of speaking ill of the dead, but we are here to honor a man whose only real God was truth. Therefore, I repeat, there were some truly difficult times. The standard of perfection by which he judged the world, and which made him in some ways the remarkable scientist that he was, made him a formidable father.

I sometimes have thought of his influence on me like the wind on the cypress trees of Big Sur. Whether I leaned into it or pulled away from it, the force of his presence shaped me. My father and I disagreed about almost everything. Politics, religion, the state of the environment, helping the homeless, you name it—we probably disagreed about it. I think it was a source of some amazement to Dad that I could think rather like him and yet arrive at diametrically opposed conclusions. But, in the end, it was the "how to think" not the "what to think" that I learned from him.

I don't remember him ever speaking directly to the subject, but from him I learned a way of being that was filled with curiosity and a love of learning. There is nothing so thrilling to me, as it was to him, as a really great, new idea. There were no un-askable questions, no problems which, given time and effort, cannot be solved, no subject taboo.

All of us can acknowledge that he was a man of extraordinary intelligence, and that the scope of his interests, and the application of his mind to the problems he encountered have changed, I think for the better, our lives. From my own perspective, I would say that, in his own unique way, my father was a deeply spiritual person. While he was a stout and confirmed advocate of orthodox atheism, he nonetheless demonstrated a reverence for life in his constant quest to understand its laws and improve its conditions, which few attain.

I remember being profoundly impressed by a rare moment he shared with me one day at the ranch in Soquel. His eyes filled with tears, and his voice choked as he described to me how he had just seen the stump of an old cherry tree, long buried under the foundation of the house. The magnificent persistence of its efforts to live, putting out one tiny pole leaf each spring in the vain hope of finding the sun, touched him deeply. That afternoon I saw a father I hadn't known was there. That moment made me understand his love of life itself, and his constant effort to expand our knowledge of it was his daily devotional.

As difficult, ornery, stubborn, blunt, and downright rude as he could sometimes be, I will miss his strength, his passion for knowledge, and his love more than I can say.

It's hard for me to believe the wind has stopped blowing.

GRETCHEN MORE OLIVER
San Francisco, California

Excerpts from the memorial tribute by Barney's eldest daughter, Karen:

All too brief a time ago, at my mother's memorial, my father hoped, half in fear, that some good things might be said of him when he died. It's as close as he came to acknowledging the lifelong emotional burden of his intellectual power. So let me now admit how difficult it often was, being close to a man who unrelentingly demanded perfection. Long before the Internet, my dad was busy flaming. In fact, he was probably the original flamer—up close and personal.

Like many so exposed, I sought a safer distance, only to inch back toward his irradiating brilliance, trying to be warmed and not burned. In time, like many of you, I came to realize that really he yelled because he truly cared. So many have praised him as friends and colleagues. Let me add to this list some special qualities I found in him as his daughter.

First, I thank my father for his imagination and care. Many children get turned upside down by their fathers in fun, but who except my dad would think to walk me all around the ceiling, stepping me around the lights? If we kids spilled feathers all over during an outdoor pillow fight, who but Dad would think to vacuum the drifting feathers off our front lawn? And who but Dad could build such a special sandbox, design such wonderful stilts, and create so beautiful and functional a drawing desk? For me? Really for me? Because he could imagine so well, I will always love good design and appreciate all things well and truly made.

Second, I feel I owe my own ability to draw at least in part to my father's amazing talent for draftsmanship. I especially remember how carefully he encouraged my developing sense of perspective. Third, I am indebted to my father's endless enthusiasm and willingness to explain, and re-explain. I know now that I have insights and familiarity with topics that few science outsiders share. Finally, I treasure my father's fearless generosity. His example has taught me what a pleasure and privilege it is to give—enthusiastically and completely—to others.

It is with gratitude that I arrive at this moment and place, where past, present, and future meet. For now, I turn to all of you, who comprised so large a part of my father's human universe. I thank you for all the years of collaboration, support, and excitement you brought him. Thank you, too, for enriching my life. Indeed, I feel I grew up partly in your company, for Dad liked nothing better than talking about your newest theories, your ongoing experiments, and your latest accomplishments.

All of us gathered in this place are part of a complicated constellation of relationships whose center of focus, my father, is gone. But we are here not simply to mourn, but to recognize our own light. Burn brightly, and learn to be your own fiercest critics. Above all, keep on realizing the possibilities that so inspired and delighted the man I knew as my father.

To Dad, who showed me the stars.

KAREN NEWTON OLIVER
Vancouver, BC, Canada